WISCONSIN

DO YOUR OWN NONPROFIT

FOURTH EDITION

WISCONSIN Do Your Own Nonprofit

Fourth Edition

Copyright © 2020 Regina Kitty Bickford. All Rights Reserved.

No rights claimed for public domain material, all rights reserved. No parts of this publication may be reproduced, stored in any retrieval system, or transmitted in any form or by any means, electronic, mechanical, recording, or otherwise, without the prior written permission of the author. Violations may be subject to civil or criminal penalties. If you need to reproduce this material, use it in a group educational or other setting, or wish to have the authors speak to or assist your organization in the 501(c) (3) process, please contact the authors at the address below.

ISBN: 978-1-63308-577-0 (paperback journal edition)

Cover Design and Interior Design by *R'tor John D. Maghuyop*

1028 S Bishop Avenue, Dept. 178
Rolla, MO 65401

www.doyourownnonprofit.com
www.taxexempt501c3.com

Printed in the United States of America

42 Books in This Series Placed in the *Top 100 Nonprofit Books of All Time* by BookAuthority.org in 2020

WISCONSIN

DO YOUR OWN NONPROFIT

The **ONLY GPS** You Need for 501(c)(3) Tax Exempt Approval

FOURTH EDITION

Dr. Kitty Bickford, DBS, CPC
and Margaret Lawing, BS Ed

CHALFANT ECKERT
PUBLISHING

ALSO BY AUTHORS

Dr. Kitty Bickford:

This is book 49 of the **Fourth Edition** of the 51-book *Do Your Own Nonprofit* state series.

*Nonprofit Touchdown:
Winning the 501(c) (3) Game Against IRS*

Margaret Lawing:

Wood's Book of Wonders: 3rd Graders Can Write

Wood's Book of Wonders: 5th Graders Can Write

*In loving memory of Kitty's wonderful husband, Jim,
who went home to be with the Lord on
May 18, 2019.*

*And to Jesus our Redeemer, Savior,
and friend who sticks closer than a brother,
Father God who watches over us and protects us,
and to the Holy Spirit who guides our paths
with His still small voice.*

Thank You All!

TABLE OF CONTENTS

ACKNOWLEDGMENTS	IX
DISCLAIMER	XI
ABOUT THE AUTHORS	XIII

PART I	INITIAL ORGANIZATIONAL SETUP	1
Chapter 1	Pay Attention: We Are Only Gonna Say This Once!	3
Chapter 2	Myths About Nonprofits	5
Chapter 3	Is 501(c)(3) Status Right for You?	19
Chapter 4	Do-It-Yourself Checklist	31
Chapter 5	Select a Business Name and Make Sure It is Available	35
Chapter 6	Get a Federal Employer Identification Number (FEIN)	39
Chapter 7	Develop a Strong Mission Statement	51
Chapter 8	Form a Board of Directors	55
Chapter 9	Crash Course on Incorporation	67
Chapter 10	Let's Incorporate and Stay Compliant!	81
Chapter 11	Let's Create Bylaws	87
Chapter 12	Develop a Conflict of Interest Policy	117
Chapter 13	Hold and Document The First Board Meeting	129

PART II	NEW ONLINE ONLY IRS FORM 1023 APPLICATION FOR TAX-EXEMPT STATUS	133
Chapter 14	Request for Recognition of Exemption	135
Chapter 15	Part I: Identification of Applicant	143
Chapter 16	Part II: Organizational Structure	149
Chapter 17	Part III: Required Provisions in Your Organizing Document	153
Chapter 18	Part IV: Your Activities	157
Chapter 19	Part V: Compensation and Other Financial Arrangements	181
Chapter 20	Part VI: Financial Data	191
Chapter 21	Part VII: Foundation Classification	207
Chapter 22	Parts VIII, IX, and X: Effective Date, Annual Filing Requirements, and Signature	217

Chapter 23	Upload Checklist	221

PART III — IRS SCHEDULES FOR TAX-EXEMPT STATUS — 225

Chapter 24	Schedule A: Churches	227
Chapter 25	Schedule B: Schools, Colleges, and Universities	235
Chapter 26	Schedule C: Hospitals and Medical Research Organizations	245
Chapter 27	Schedule D: Section 509(a) (3) Supporting Organizations	255
Chapter 28	Schedule E: Effective Date	267
Chapter 29	Schedule F: Low-Income Housing	273
Chapter 30	Schedule G: Successors to Other Organizations	277
Chapter 31	Schedule H: Organizations Providing Scholarships, Fellowships, Educational Loans, or Other Educational Grants to Individuals and Private Foundations Requesting Advance Approval of Individual Grant Procedures	281

PART IV — FORM 1023-EZ — 291

Chapter 32	Form 1023-EZ: Streamlined Application	293

PART V — SPECIAL FEATURE BY GRANT GURU JUDY HANNA — 301

Chapter 33	The Art of Grant Writing for Your Nonprofit	303

PART VI — SPECIAL CIRCUMSTANCES — 313

Chapter 34	Automatic Revocation of 501(c) (3) Status	315

PART VII — FOLLOW-UP TASKS — 319

Chapter 35	Annual Filing Requirements with IRS	321
Chapter 36	Apply for Nonprofit Standard Mail Rates	327

SUMMARY	329
APPENDIX A	331
APPENDIX B	337

ACKNOWLEDGMENTS

We serve a God who makes the impossible *totally* possible. In our own strength, we can do nothing, but we can do all things through Christ who strengthens us. Our Christian walks have seen many twists and turns, each one more exciting than the last, and so much better than we could have dreamed up alone. Thank you, God, for your marvelous direction. Thank you, Holy Spirit, for that still small voice of guidance to keep us on the right paths. Thank you, Jesus, for going to the cross in our stead so that we can have eternal life in heaven, and life abundantly in the meantime. It just doesn't get any better than that!

DISCLAIMER

While the information contained in this book was prepared with best efforts and in good faith, the publisher and authors make no representations or warranties concerning the accuracy or completeness of the contents herein.

This work (in any electronic or digital form or any other printed material form) is not intended for use as a source of legal, accounting, tax, or financial advice. If advice concerning legal, accounting, tax, financial, or any other professional advice is needed, seek the services of a qualified, duly licensed, and competent professional.

The contents of this work reflect the views and opinions of the authors. The authors and publisher have made their best efforts to produce a high quality, informative, and helpful course on getting approved for Section 501(c) (3) tax-exempt status by the Internal Revenue Service (IRS). However, they make no representations or warranties of any kind about the completeness and accuracy of the contents of the course. Any slights of people and organizations are unintentional.

Neither the authors nor the publisher accept any liability of any kind for any losses or damages caused or alleged to be caused, directly or indirectly, from using the information contained in this book. Every individual must make his or her own decisions. Although this book describes the experiences of the authors, it in no way guarantees similar successes for others. Every effort has been made to ensure that this publication is free from errors and problems.

ABOUT THE AUTHORS

MARGARET LAWING

*The Lord is my rock, and my fortress,
and my deliverer; my God, my strength, in whom
I will trust; my buckler, and the horn of my salvation,
and my high tower.*

Psalm 18:2 (KJV)

Margaret has been setting up tax-exempt nonprofits from concept to 501(c) (3) approval and subsequent compliance for five years. She has completed hundreds of IRS packages and dealt with government agencies in all 50 states. A valuable member of the TaxExempt501.com team, Margaret monitors and tracks changes in state and federal government regulations, forms, and procedures, as well as creates 501(c) (3) organizations for anxious philanthropists ready to dive into their missions, but not ready to do the paperwork to get there.

Margaret has two Bachelor of Science degrees from Missouri State University: one in Early Childhood Education and one in Elementary Education. She is one class away from a Master of Education degree in Early Childhood Education. She taught third and fifth grade at elementary schools on Fort Leonard Wood Army Base in St. Roberts, Missouri. She has been very active in Head Start, serving on the policy council and parent committees. She was named Volunteer of the Year twice for her continuous efforts to ensure children learn as early in life as possible before she became part of the Head Staff of educators.

Margaret has a love for children and has given back for five years through KidCare America, an afterschool program for at-risk children. She is a mentor and carves out time in her busy life to work with those kids three days a week.

Mother of four and grandmother of two, Margaret is Mother Earth and a devoted parent, never missing a ball game, choir presentation, or any other event important to her children. When she became a mom, she decided to put her children's needs at the top of the list, and it has worked out well for her family. She will soon celebrate her 22nd wedding anniversary.

DR. KITTY BICKFORD

*Thy word have I hid in mine heart,
that I might not sin against thee.*

PSALM 119:11 (KJV)

Dr. Kitty Bickford lives, breathes, and eats nonprofits 24/6 (Sunday is the Lord's Day). She owns *Tax Exempt 501c3, LLC* (taxexempt501c3.com) and is an independent contractor for *Harbor Compliance*, both national incorporation services with great reputations and excellent services. She has completed over one thousand five hundred 501(c) (3) packages for IRS with no rejects, and contracts affordable follow-up consulting services to new nonprofits that need guidance for the first year as well as their first nonprofit tax return completed for them. Kitty is a Certified Professional Coach (CPC) for nonprofit business leaders and coaches nonprofit executives to grow their organizations.

MILITARY CAREER AND FAMILY

Dr. Kitty Bickford is a Christian woman who spent from 1979–1989 in the United States Air Force. The last five years of her military career were spent as a Master Instructor and On-the-Job Training Advisor for Air Training Command, achieving the noncommissioned officer rank of E-6 (Technical Sergeant).

In 1984, she met and eventually married Master Sergeant Jim Bickford, who was twenty-two years her senior. They were happy together for 35 years, enjoying four children, fourteen grandchildren (one with God), and now six great-grandchildren.

TEACHING AND MISSIONARY WORK

After leaving the military, Kitty continued her teaching career, first teaching college, then she retired from teaching public school. In 2006, Kitty was selected as ING Corporation's *Unsung Hero* for Missouri for educational innovation. She has made almost 350 microfinance loans in 80 countries to the world's poor through Kiva.org for mostly disadvantaged women. These loans allow women to start their own businesses and become self-sufficient.

Kitty supports missionaries to Zimbabwe, Zambia, and Ukraine. She was awarded the 2013 Spirit of Rolla Award in recognition of significant achievement and/or lifetime contribution to the spirit of giving. She holds undergraduate degrees in Educational Administration, Behavioral Science, and Criminal Justice, completed the undergraduate teacher certification program for Missouri, holds a graduate degree in Psychology, has studied Special Education at the doctorate level, and holds a Doctorate in Biblical Studies. She is currently completing the first Master of Arts Degree program in the United States in Grant Writing, Management, and Evaluation at Concordia University Chicago.

PHILANTHROPY

In 2005, Kitty sponsored an orphaned child in Eswatini (formerly Swaziland), Africa. When she went to visit him in 2012, she was disappointed to find that the organization she trusted to care for him lacked the integrity she expected. Upon returning to the United States, God led her to start a nonprofit organization that would not be corrupt and would actually do some good for hungry kids and vulnerable families.

Kitty soon found that the 501(c) (3) process was either long and complicated or very expensive. She chose the long and complicated option because spending up to $7,000 for an attorney to do paperwork seemed counterproductive. After much study, questioning, and hard work, IRS approved *Pasture Valley Children Missions* on the first try. Elated, she thanked God that the process was over so she could get down to work feeding children. To her surprise, God spoke to her spirit and told her to write a book for others who want to start nonprofits on a shoestring. She wrote *Nonprofit Touchdown: Winning the 501(c) (3) Game Against IRS*. It was 370 pages long, a national edition that covered all 50 states and DC. She later decided that individual books for each state would be easier for the reader to use. That is why the *Do Your Own Nonprofit* 51-book state series was born. Now in fourth editions, the *Do Your Own Nonprofit* series has helped thousands of people from all walks of life to start and run successful nonprofits. In 2020, 42 books of the 51-book series were named in the **Top 100 Nonprofit Books of All Time** by BookAuthority.org.

BENEVOLANCE

Dr. Bickford started *BenevoLance* (EIN 81-0687426), an international 501(c) (3) that provides intervention for struggling families, elderly and handicapped people, and those in danger due to abuse in the United States, the Philippines, Jamaica, and Serbia, with plans to expand worldwide over time.

BenevoLance fosters global partnerships through networking with other nonprofits, businesses, and other food banks to enrich, support, and enhance the lives of disadvantaged individuals, children, and assist communities through mentoring, raising awareness, and providing tangible assistance to relieve suffering and to increase individual abilities to become self-sustaining. The nonprofit provides needed food and establishes food banks and food distribution centers, shelters, access to medical care, clothing, and education to the needy. They help veterans in need and provide assistive technologies for handicapped individuals. *BenevoLance* helps individuals, families, and communities around the world with sustainable development projects, economic development projects, obtaining clean water and affordable energy, access to improved educational opportunities, job training and internship programs, as well as cultural exchange, disaster relief, and humanitarian aid. *BenevoLance* is the culminating outcome of years of philanthropy, and Kitty wants to touch 10,000+ lives in her lifetime through assistance provided by this nonprofit.

WORLD DEVELOPMENT CENTER

Kitty recently took over management of World Development Center, a 501(c)(3) that seeks to narrow the development gap for third-world countries. It is her vision to collaborate with African and Asian stakeholders to bring improved education, training, and entrepreneur programs into being.

WHAT'S NEXT?

We live in an international culture run by technology. People all over the world have skills and talents to share. Several reputable online venues put buyers of talent together with the talented, but in Kitty's mind, they charge too much for the privilege. She is working on *HumaniTen, Good SamariTens, Free-ployment.org,* and *E-ployment.org* online marketplaces for buyers and sellers to do business around the world. These services, similar to Fiverr, Freelancer, Upwork, Guru, and others, will charge *reasonable* fees and give 10% of the profit to nonprofits to fund specific project needs. She plans to help her client base initially with

WISCONSIN

funding for their projects and expand to other organizations over time.

Her goals for these upcoming marketplaces include multiple efforts for humans and humanity:

Build: 100 schools in poverty-stricken rural areas of the world, where children cannot afford transportation to get to school and live too far to walk;

Send: 1,000 bright kids to college who would not otherwise be able to go;

Fund: 10,000 nonprofits to make their projects come to life;

Create opportunities for: 100,000 entrepreneurs who have no market for their skills;

Feed: 1,000,000 people, many of them children, who regularly go to bed hungry.

Ambitious goals? YEP! To God be the glory, because she could not do any of those things in her own strength, but she can do all things through Christ who strengthens her (Philippians 4:13).

Pasture Valley's documentary, *"In Faith We Grow"* won best documentary at the Hollywood International Moving Picture Film Festival. See it at www.infaithwegrow.com

THE STORY OF PASTURE VALLEY CHILDREN'S HOME

PART I
INITIAL ORGANIZATIONAL SETUP

CHAPTER 1

PAY ATTENTION

WE ARE ONLY GONNA SAY THIS ONCE!

"If God called us to a task, He will then qualify us for the job."

—Jack Hyles

On January 31, 2020, IRS changed everything again: New forms, new procedures, new time frames. Keeping up with IRS and state requirements and changes feels like a full-time job.

This page is not a sales pitch; it is an offer to relieve you of the logistics of setting up your nonprofit. We stay busy all the time and are not trying to generate new business. Instead, we are offering to make it easier for you if you don't want to become a subject matter specialist on tax-exempt law. Many people have the heart for philanthropic work but get bogged down in the details of the paperwork and quit or never get started. If that describes you, then you may want to hear this!

If you would prefer not to have to learn the details of setup so that you can just get to the mission without the paperwork hassle, consider contacting Tax Exempt 501c3, LLC to do this work. Our fees are *very* reasonable compared to other services, we are normally done in one to two weeks or less, guarantee our results (100% IRS acceptance with no rejects ever), are insured for errors and omissions (with no claims ever), and have a track record of over 1,500 happy clients (with no dissatisfied clients). If you want us to do this work, PLEASE DO NOT DO ANYTHING! Everything is included in our services. It is easier for us and cheaper for you if we do it all so that we do not have to fix anything that was inadvertently filed incorrectly.

We are not going to say it again, but we wanted you to know that the service is available if you want it.

Tax Exempt 501c3, LLC

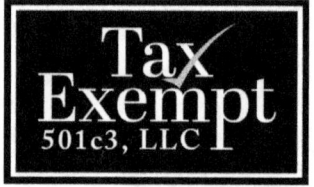

Dr. Kitty Bickford, DBS, CPC
PO Box 1665, Rolla, MO 65402
(573) 201-4832
kbickford@centurylink.net
www.taxexempt501c3.com

Margaret Lawing, BS Ed
PO Box 1665, Rolla, MO 65402
(417) 293-6834
mlawing242@gmail.com
www.taxexempt501c3.com

Tax Exempt 501c3, LLC

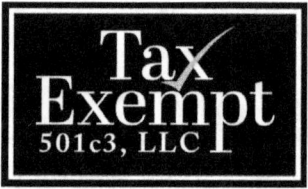

CHAPTER 2

MYTHS ABOUT NONPROFITS

"Twenty years from now you will be more disappointed by the things that you didn't do than by the ones you did do."

—MARK TWAIN

Pasture Valley Children Missions *was founded by Dr. Kitty Bickford to provide a hand up, not a handout, to orphans and vulnerable families in Swaziland, Africa.*

Starting and running a 501(c)(3) tax-exempt nonprofit is a lot of work, and not everyone is cut out for it. Some go into the venture with false assumptions and myths and later find out they didn't understand what they were getting themselves into. Let's examine some of those myths.

Myth: *Nonprofit* and *tax-exempt* mean the same thing.
Truth: *The state grants nonprofit status. IRS gives tax-exempt status.* Once you get nonprofit status, you can go about your mission and announce to the world that your organization is a legitimate state-approved nonprofit. However, if you do not also go the step further and apply for federal (IRS) *tax-exempt* status, your nonprofit is not eligible for tax deductions for those who make donations (churches are the exception), and the nonprofit does not qualify for most foundation grants.
Moral of this Myth: Apply for federal 501(c)(3) tax-exempt status if you want donations to be tax deductible, and you want to apply for foundation grants.

Myth: I own my nonprofit.
Truth: No, you don't. Nonprofits are not owned. They are run by boards of directors who call the shots and make the decisions. If you are not on the board, you have no control or input into the business of the nonprofit. If you get voted off the board, you are just out. The organization continues without you, even though you may have started it and invested blood, sweat, and tears into building it.
Moral of this Myth: Be very careful who you let on your board of directors.

Myth: I am going to convert my for-profit business to a nonprofit business.

Truth: Conversion is not as simple or easy as it sounds. In most states, you have to dissolve the for-profit business and reapply as a nonprofit. Some states have statutory waiting periods between the two. Also, when you complete the process, you no longer have access to the revenues of the for-profit business. The newly formed nonprofit is run by a board of directors who must use the revenue for approved nonprofit purposes only. And remember, you can get voted off your board and if that happens, you lose your business.

Moral of this Myth: Consider keeping your for-profit business (and the profit it makes). Start a nonprofit to handle the philanthropic aspects of your charitable work. *The two must remain separate on paper.* The nonprofit is allowed to benefit from the for-profit, but the for-profit is not allowed to benefit from the nonprofit. If you keep the for-profit business and start a nonprofit, you can donate money to the nonprofit (and take the tax deduction) and share assets (equipment, furniture, building space, etc.) with the nonprofit, but maintain unregulated use of the for-profit revenues without board or IRS oversight. You cannot have the same name for the nonprofit as you have for the for-profit business, but you can have a similar name, or come up with a different name. For example, suppose you had a thriving for-profit educational tutoring business called *Education Ventures*. You could name your nonprofit that tutors kids for free *Education Adventures*.

Myth: I am going to set up my nonprofit as a limited liability corporation (LLC).

Truth: A few states allow nonprofits to register as LLCs. However, IRS does not allow it for 501(c) (3) tax-exempt status. Why?

Because an LLC is a for-profit entity, and a nonprofit is a not-for-profit entity. The two do not mix. The only exception is if every member of the LLC is a nonprofit organization.

Moral of this Myth: Choose a corporation as the nonprofit entity. Fewer headaches, more protection for board members against personal liability, and no IRS rejections for filing the wrong entity.

Myth: I am starting a foundation to give out school supplies to kids who cannot afford them. I can't wait to see their little faces when I give them new backpacks and markers!

Truth: Foundations cannot provide direct aid to individuals, but public charities can. Although foundations and public charities are both classified as types of 501(c) (3) nonprofits, they are not the same. Many foundations are set up by corporations or wealthy philanthropists who want to give money to worthwhile causes instead of giving it to IRS for income tax. Because foundations can (and often are) run by families or specific corporations, they are more highly regulated and operate under different rules than public charities. For example, donations to foundations are only deductible up to 30% of adjusted gross income. For public charities, it is 60% of adjusted gross income. There are some specific exceptions, but that is the general rule.

Foundations must give away a percentage of revenues every year (with some exceptions) while public charities have no such requirements. Foundations can only give funding to other 501(c) approved organizations and must prove due diligence to IRS for every grant they give. Foundations demonstrate due diligence by getting copies of the organization's IRS approval documentation to prove the organization is tax-exempt, and a copy of the most recent nonprofit tax return to show that the organization is in good standing with IRS. Organizations that have not filed their first nonprofit tax return with IRS typically do not get approved for grants. Foundations don't want to get into trouble with IRS for not being diligent.

School kids needing backpacks do not have IRS credentials or nonprofit tax returns, and foundations cannot give out school supplies directly to children. They work through public charities or other nonprofits by giving them grants to buy school supplies and hope that is what the organizations actually do with the money. Public charities must exercise prudence but are allowed to work directly with people when performing their missions so that public charities can give out backpacks and markers directly to kids. If you want to work directly with people, start a public charity, not a foundation.

Many organizations choose to use the word *foundation* in their names when they are actually public charities. Although IRS allows it, confusion sometimes happens. For example, when a public charity applies to a foundation for a grant but has the word *foundation* in the organization's name, the foundation giving the grant may wonder why another foundation is applying to them for money. Foundations generally give money, not ask for grants. When there is only so much money available for grants, foundations must find ways to weed out applicants so that they can pick the most worthwhile causes to fund. Don't give them a reason to weed out your organization by calling yourself a foundation when you are not. Think of it this way: Would you call yourself an apple if you were hanging on an orange tree? Both are fruits, but that is where the similarity ends. It is the same with public charities and foundations. Both are 501(c) (3) tax-exempt nonprofits, but that is where the similarity ends.

Moral of this Myth: Choose your status carefully. Public Charity status is the gold standard of 501(c)(3) tax-exempt nonprofits. Foundations work well if you plan to have all family on your board and you plan to do your own funding or fund through a corporation you own or control.

Myth: I am going to be president of my nonprofit and make $100,000 a year!

Truth: It is not *your* nonprofit, and most nonprofit boards are manned by volunteers (especially small nonprofits just starting out) who receive no compensation except for reimbursement of reasonable costs associated with fulfilling their roles as board members. When you get big enough to have salaries, the board votes on the jobs that need to be filled, the hours, the pay, and the job descriptions. The board hires people who work *for* the board and report *to* the board. If the board hires you as a program director or some other function you are most qualified for, you are not being paid in your capacity as a board member, and you cannot vote on your pay. When the board vote starts, you should leave the room to avoid a conflict of interest. If you are on the board and going to be an employee, you have no input into your salary as a hired employee of the organization.

Moral of this Myth: Roll up your sleeves and get ready to do a lot of hard work to grow your organization to the point that you can draw a salary as a program director or employee of the board. Don't expect to get rich being the president of a fledgling nonprofit.

Myth: I will put all family members on the board of directors, and we will control the organization.

Truth: You can put just family members on the board, but IRS will look at the composition of family members. If more than half of the board is made up of related people, there is a chance that IRS will flag your tax-exempt application for follow-up by an IRS agent, and your request for approval as a public charity may be reclassified as a foundation. Is that written anywhere? No, but call IRS at 877-829-5500 and ask what percentage of a nonprofit board for a public charity can be related. The answer will be something like, "Although we do not specify in statutes, we want to see less than half the board made up of related members." Additional queries will reveal that IRS frowns on public charities that are controlled by related people. Public charities exist for the benefit of the public, not for the benefit of family members. You can always add members later and report those changes to IRS in your annual report.

Moral of this Myth: To avoid any complications in processing your application, make sure that at least 50% of your board of directors are unrelated.

Myth: I didn't apply to IRS for 501(c) (3) tax-exempt status, so I don't have to file federal annual nonprofit tax returns.

Truth: All nonprofits (except churches) must file annual tax returns with IRS. Over 650,000 nonprofits have made the mistake of not filing required tax returns and have had their present (or future!) tax-exempt status revoked. When the deadline to file for the third consecutive year comes and goes, IRS computers make a note that an organization is automatically revoked from 501(c) (3) status, even if that organization has never applied. If the nonprofit later applies, an IRS agent will review the application, approve it, and put the info in the IRS computer, which will spit out an approval letter. But then the organization will get a later letter that says their 501(c) (3) was automatically revoked for failure to file taxes for three consecutive years. To get the status back, the nonprofit must reapply and give IRS good reasons to reinstate the organization and pay the filing fee again. The exceptions are churches.

Moral of this Myth: If you have not filed your nonprofit taxes, do not apply for federal 501(c) (3) status until you catch up (and are sure IRS has the returns recorded in their computer system). If many years have gone by, you might just start a new nonprofit from scratch and let the other nonprofit die a quiet death in a lonely corner of the closet where the paperwork is stored. It is sometimes easier and wiser to start over rather than go through the hassles of resurrecting a dead paper trail of a nonprofit that has delinquent filings with the state or IRS. Once you get reinstated by the feds, then many states want missing filings as well. It can turn into an expensive and time-consuming process to get caught up for the years you missed. Because nonprofit records are public records, it might be easier to pick a new name and start over, so that your organization has a clean paper trail.

Myth: Nonprofits are not allowed to make a profit from their activities.

Truth: Of course they can! How can a business stay in business if it does not make a profit? According to the *Council of Nonprofits*, less than 10% of revenues come from individual donations to nonprofits. The breakdown looks something like this: 30% of revenues from government sources, 50% from fees for services provided by the nonprofit, and the rest from foundation grants, investments, corporate donations, and other sources. Yes, nonprofits can and should make a profit. If they do not generate revenue above expenses, how can they continue to exist or expand in the future?

Nonprofit organizations can make a profit; they just cannot spend it to benefit individuals unless those individuals are part of their target mission. A nonprofit can buy a new pair of shoes for an orphan, but not a new pair of shoes for the board president.

Moral of this Myth: Plan for and expect to have excess revenue over expenses. The alternative is not self-sustaining.

Myth: If we are running our nonprofit efficiently, our indirect and administrative overhead should be small.

Truth: Not necessarily. If you are running a tutoring program for at-risk kids, you might get volunteers willing to do the work, but if you are running a mental health facility for war veterans with Post Traumatic Stress Disorder (PTSD), you need trained therapists and credentialed counselors. If you are running a nonprofit charter school, teachers need to buy groceries and pay mortgages just as public school teachers do. Skilled professionals cannot afford to work for free; you have to pay them reasonable wages for the skills they provide to your nonprofit. It is possible that your highest expense could be salaries. That doesn't mean you are doing anything wrong. As long as the wages paid are comparable to other nonprofits of similar size and mission, and as long as the work is getting done, write the check!

Moral of this Myth: Spend what is prudent to provide the best services you can to fulfill your mission. Get the best people you can afford and treat them well so they will want to stay and grow with the organization.

Myth: Grants are easy to get if you have 501(c)(3) status.

Truth: Just because you apply for a grant does not mean you are going to get it. New nonprofits with no track record of success are not likely to get grant money. Many think they can hire a hotshot grant writer who will bring in big bucks. The truth is that there are only so many grant dollars available, and grant makers choose the organizations with proven success that have the most potential to have the biggest impact. New nonprofits often have not reached a competitive level yet. Board members often blame grant writers because they didn't get the grants, but in reality, they should have channeled their efforts into creating a group of supporters to make repeated contributions instead of chasing elusive grant money.

To write a big grant (meaning $100K - $1,000,000+), the grant writer will spend weeks to months preparing the grant package. Grants are highly competitive and even leaving out one tiny detail in a grant package can cause the grant to be denied. Grant writers often charge a flat fee to start ($5K – 25K), and then a percentage of the grant, often 10%. That creates a problem for many organizations because most grants have a stipulation that you cannot pay grant writers from the proceeds of the grant. That means that the organization must pay the grant writer out of general operating funds. If those funds are not available, the organization cannot hire the grant writer. If the organization does not get the grant, they have already spent the flat fee, which somewhat compensated the grant writer for preparing the submission.

Moral of this Myth: Establish a proven track record of success before applying for grants. Select grant writers carefully. You get what you pay for. Pick grant writers with multiple proven successes and expect to pay good money for their talents and skills. Verify their prior grants with the organizations that were approved. Check with the organization and also with the grant maker. If the grant writer will not give you organization and foundation names and amounts, move on. Many grant writers will say they are protecting the privacy of the organizations they worked with. Not true! Everything about grants is public record and can be verified on both the nonprofit recipient's tax return and the grant maker's tax return. They are both public records. The truth might be that the grant writer has no success and doesn't want to tell you. Good grant writers are worth their hire and can mean the difference in an organization growing – or just maintaining the status quo. Don't blame the grant writer if you do not get funded. Many variables go into the selection process, and lots of the considerations have nothing to do with the grant writer.

Myth: We can expand our mission later when we have more resources.

Truth: IRS and the state approve you for a particular mission. If you choose to expand it, you have to report the change to IRS when you file your annual tax return. At that point, IRS can approve or deny your request. Kitty ran into that problem with *Pasture Valley Children Missions*. It was set up to work with orphans, orphanages, and vulnerable families in Swaziland, Africa. Unfortunately, we were only able to find four grants that dealt with both orphans and Swaziland. That was not an enormous pool of potential funding when compared to the size of the HIV/AIDS orphan problem in that country. After a few years, we wanted to expand the mission to other countries and to include other philanthropic pursuits (shelters for abused women, economic development projects, water treatment and access, etc.). Our mission did not cover those things, and we had no authority to pursue philanthropy in the United States. To fix the situation, she started a second nonprofit, *BenevoLance*, and made the mission extremely broad for this second nonprofit so that we had room to grow without having to start a third nonprofit.

Moral of this Myth: Write your mission wider than your current narrow focus regarding geographic location and activities so that five years down the road, you don't have to go back to IRS and start over or deal with red tape to get approval to expand. Write a broad mission now as you get started, so you have the option to grow in different directions later. Just because you are approved for a certain mission does not mean you have to be working on that specific mission at any given time. You can work on what your board decides is the best focus for the organization at the current time. Additional things you are approved for can wait for the future. You are not obligated to pursue every aspect of your mission simultaneously. Think big and apply big the first time!

Myth: I need a huge board of directors (or I don't need a board at all, just me).

Truth: About half the states require one board member minimum, the other half require at least three. Only New Hampshire requires five. However, just about every state specifies in their statutes which positions need to be filled and what combinations are not allowed. For example, many states prohibit the board president from also being the secretary or treasurer. Even if the state does not specify, IRS scrutinizes any board of less than three unrelated board members. If you call them (and we have several times to see if we got the same answer every time) at 877-829-5500 and ask what the minimum number of board members is, you will get this answer: "IRS statutes do not specify a minimum number of board members."

Next, ask, "How many board members does IRS want to see so that the number of board members is not an issue?"

The answer: "Three unrelated board members or five if two are related."

Moral of this Myth: Pick at least three unrelated board members and be done with it, or at least four, but preferably five members if two are related. Board members do not have to be in the same state, and if your mission is international, they don't even have to be in the same country.

Myth: I can use the money for my nonprofit for anything I want.
Truth: No, you cannot. The Board of Directors approves all expenditures, and each expense must relate to the nonprofit mission. You cannot use the money to pay your electric bill or car insurance just because you generated the income. All nonprofit revenues belong to the nonprofit and must be used for the approved nonprofit mission.
Moral of this Myth: Make sure you have other income to sustain your needs before deciding to pursue your nonprofit mission full time. If you are a salaried employee of the nonprofit and are performing needed functions on behalf of the nonprofit, the board can pay you reasonable compensation for services actually rendered. You are not getting paid to be on the board; you are getting paid in a second capacity as an employee of the board.

Myth: If I give a building, vehicle, computer, book I wrote, or whatever to the nonprofit and later close the nonprofit, I can just change the copyright, deed, or title back into my name again, or take the property back.
Truth: When an asset of any kind becomes the legal property of a nonprofit, it can never go back to the person who donated it. If the nonprofit closes, the asset must be given to another nonprofit, or the court can decide the disposition of the asset. In no case can it go to an individual.
Moral of this Myth: If you want to retain a claim on physical property, loan it to the nonprofit, do not deed it or gift it. Once it is gone, it is gone forever, and you have no claim to it. If instead you choose to loan it, the organization gets the benefit, but you still own it. That includes books. Keep your book copyright in your own name, and donate royalties

if and when you want to, or give the right for the nonprofit to use your intellectual property, but don't give your book to the nonprofit. You cannot get the rights back later.

Myth: We are going to start a hybrid social enterprise organization and get 501(c)(3) status.
Truth: Hybrid organizations are part for-profit, part nonprofit. Some states have approved them, but IRS is not likely to approve this type of organization. For one thing, it is too new, and laws have not caught up. For another, for-profit organizations are not eligible for 501(c)(3) tax-exempt status.
Moral of this Myth: Don't waste your time and money. Follow the path that gets you approved!

Myth: I am going to get 501(c)(3) status to grow medical marijuana.
Truth: IRS cannot rule on cannabis-related efforts. Although growing medical marijuana is legal in some states, it illegal at federal level, so IRS will not rule on any 501(c) application that involves cannabis.
Moral of this Myth: Don't apply for 501(c)(3) or 501(c)(6) if your nonprofit has to do with cannabis. It will not be approved.

CHAPTER 3

IS 501(C) (3) STATUS RIGHT FOR YOU?

*I can do all things through Christ
who strengthens me.*

—Philippians 4:13 NKJV

STEP-BY-STEP INSTRUCTIONS

So, you have this great idea for a nonprofit floating around in your head, but just don't know what to do with it. If so, you are not alone. Many people want to make a difference in the world, but they either don't know how, can't afford an attorney to set it up, or they get buried in the mountain of paperwork needed to get 501(c)(3) tax-exempt status.

We want to make the setup easy for you. We know from personal experience the areas that are the most difficult (so much so that many people give up because it is just too hard). **This book gives you step-by-step instructions on what to do in the correct order for your state,** how to do it, where to do it, how long it takes, who to call, and what it costs. Just that information saves much time and aggravation. But that is not all you get.

ASK US 3 SPECIFIC QUESTIONS

You get to ask us three specific questions during your 501(c)(3) project. It is our way of saying thank you for buying this book. Just go to *www.doyourownnonprofit.com* or *www.taxexempt501c3.com* and contact us, or call or email. We are glad to help you! But that is not all. We have gone the extra mile and given you great resources we wish we would have had that will remove the most frustrating part of the tax-exempt process: paperwork!

FILL-IN-THE-BLANK STATE TEMPLATES

Does the thought of preparing articles of organization, bylaws, conflict of interest policies, and board meeting minutes make you nervous? Your stomach queasy? Fill you with dread? Make you want to forget the whole idea?

Kitty had the same feelings when she started Pasture Valley Children Missions, so she hired a $300-an-hour attorney on your behalf to develop fill-in-the-blank templates of the documents that were cumbersome and time-consuming. These templates are available word-for-word in this book if you want to type them out. If you prefer to download them already typed, you can go to *www.doyourownnonprofit.org*, click on State Templates, and for a small fee, you can download the documents in Word (PDF available upon email request). The fee for a whole stack of documents is $19.95 and the money goes to support Pasture Valley Children Missions, we do not keep any of it. You can do the state and in-house paperwork in 30 minutes with full assurance of the legal integrity of the documents. If you prefer to type out the documents, you can do so right out of the book and spend nothing.

> **You can do the state and in-house paperwork in 30 minutes with full assurance of the legal integrity of the documents.**

EXAMPLES OF APPROVED NONPROFITS

A picture is worth a thousand words, so we researched other 501(c) (3) organizations, and in Appendix A, you will find links to their paperwork. Find an organization like the one you are starting and study their federal application before filling out yours. IRS has gone to mandatory online applications effective January 31, 2020. The examples will help you figure out how you might answer the online questions.

We hope that the benefits of the book, website, templates, and access to paperwork from other nonprofits make your experience easy, and we hope you will contact us if you run into trouble so we can figure it out together. Now let's look at the benefits of starting a tax-exempt organization.

BENEFITS OF 501(C) (3) TAX-EXEMPT STATUS

People pursue 501(c) (3) status for different reasons. In addition to the intangible rewards (satisfaction, doing the right thing, helping people, feeling good about your efforts), there are tangible reasons to pursue your mission as a tax-exempt organization.

Below are a few of the more tangible benefits:

- Tax deductions to contributors
- Limited liability
- Perpetual existence and permanence
- Eligibility for grants
- Tax-exempt purchasing power in some states
- Reduced postage
- Discounted internet service provider costs
- Public service announcements on the radio and other media at little or no charge

Getting to the approval process with the Internal Revenue Service (IRS) requires that you complete many steps along the way. This state guide is designed to get you there quickly with no unnecessary steps, wasted effort, or scratching your head wondering what to do next. The best part is that you do not have to hire an attorney to do the paperwork for you. If you can follow a checklist and simple instructions, you can complete the requirements to get tax-exempt status.

IRS states that for an organization to be tax-exempt, it must be "organized and operated exclusively for exempt purposes set forth in Section 501(c) (3)..."

Those exempt purposes include:

- Charitable
- Religious
- Educational
- Scientific
- Literary
- Testing for public safety (although contributions are not tax deductible)
- Fostering national or international sports competition
- Preventing cruelty to children and animals

IRS DIRECTIVE

Here's how the IRS looks at the status:

> ... the term charitable is used in its generally accepted legal sense and includes relief of the poor, the distressed, or the underprivileged; advancement of religion; advancement of education or science; erecting or maintaining public buildings, monuments, or works; lessening the burdens of government; lessening neighborhood tensions; eliminating prejudice and discrimination; defending human and civil rights secured by

law; and combating community deterioration and juvenile delinquency.

CHURCHES AND RELIGIOUS ENTITIES

Religious nonprofits are harder to pinpoint but form a class of exemption with some commonalities. If it looks like a church, acts like a church, operates like a church, and feels like a church, then it is probably a church. However, a church must have:

- distinct religious beliefs and denomination
- a location to meet
- a schedule of services on a regular basis
- a stable group of people that make up the congregation

Proof of the above aspects may be required to get the exemption. IRS defines *church* to also include synagogues, temples, and mosques.

In the list below are those organizations that do not have to file the 501(c)(3) application as they are automatically exempt:

- Churches
- Interchurch organizations of the local units of the church
- Conventions or associations of churches
- Integrated auxiliaries of a church (such as a men's or women's organization)
- Religious school
- Mission society
- Youth group

Churches are automatically exempt without filing 501(c)(3) paperwork with IRS. They just have to make sure they mark the church box when they get their federal employer identification number. Many churches still choose to file for 501(c)(3) tax-exempt status because it assures their tithers and donors that contributions qualify for tax deductions. Church auxiliary organizations can fall under the church umbrella for 501(c) (3) purposes under certain circumstances. The benefit of being under that umbrella is that there is no requirement to file an annual tax return with IRS.

Many other religious organizations that are not churches under IRS codes may still qualify for tax-exempt status as religious organizations, but unlike churches, they have to file annual information tax returns. These might include:

- Mission organizations
- Speakers' organizations
- Nondenominational ministries
- Ecumenical organizations
- Faith-based social agencies
- Evangelistic ministries

EDUCATIONAL ORGANIZATIONS

The IRS definition of educational organizations includes schools at all levels from elementary to college and beyond, as well as trade schools, correspondence schools, and schools that provide education through media such as internet, television, and radio. Some other types of organizations that may not be immediately obvious as educational may qualify for tax-exemption as educational organizations:

- Museums
- Zoos
- Planetariums
- Symphony orchestras
- Organizations that conduct public discussion groups, forums, panels, and lectures

In addition, nonprofit daycare centers and youth sports organizations may qualify as educational tax-exempt organizations.

SCIENTIFIC ORGANIZATIONS

Scientific organizations that want 501(c) (3) status must demonstrate that their research is in the public interest. That is done by using the results (including patents, copyrights, processes, or formulas) in nondiscriminatory ways for the public good. The research can be for science, education, publications available to the public, curing disease, or helping attract new industry to an area. Research does not include product testing.

LITERARY ORGANIZATIONS

Literary organizations seeking 501(c) (3) status must be able to show that any sales or publishing they do is related to their tax-exempt purpose.

AMATEUR ATHLETIC ORGANIZATIONS

Amateur athletic organizations fall into two categories:

1. Those that promote national or international amateur sports competition but do not supply facilities or equipment, and
2. Those that exclusively develop athletes and/or conduct national or international amateur sports competition and provide facilities and equipment, even though the membership is local or regional.

ORGANIZATIONS THAT PREVENT CRUELTY TO CHILDREN AND ANIMALS

Organizations that seek to prevent cruelty to children and animals may:

- Try to protect children forced into dangerous jobs
- Advocate alternatives to child abuse
- Seek humane treatment for laboratory animals
- Assist in animal population control
- Provide shelters for abused animals
- Make other attempts to reduce cruelty to animals or children

SEPARATE ENTITY FROM FOUNDERS

Your organization must be set up and organized in such a way that IRS recognizes it as a separate entity from its founders. In other words, the people who start it do not own it. It is not their organization; it is separate and perpetual and will survive even if the founders do not. For this reason, be careful not to call yourself the owner of a 501(c)(3) organization (especially when dealing with IRS). You can start the organization. You can be on the board. You can be president of the board. You can be an advisor to the board. However, you cannot be an owner. A tax-exempt organization is *NOT* owned. One individual does not operate it; it is normally governed and run by a board of directors, and there are distinct rules about the number and relationships of those on the board (covered in a later chapter).

> You can be on the board. You can be president of the board. You can be an advisor to the board. However, you cannot be an owner.

NOT FOR PRIVATE INTEREST

Section 501(c) (3) status *DOES NOT* apply to organizations created for the benefit of private interests or those that do not receive a substantial part of their income from the general public or the government. You cannot get 501(c) (3) status so that you or your family or friends can benefit from the tax-exempt status. It must benefit the public to be eligible for 501(c) (3). Your organization also cannot be set up to benefit a specific person or organization. You cannot participate in political campaigns directly or indirectly at any level, but you can have educational meetings, create educational materials, and appear before government bodies. You may not participate in illegal activities.

> **Your organization also cannot be set up to benefit a specific person or organization.**

The following types of organizations **DO NOT** qualify for 501(c) (3) status:

- 501(c) (1) organizations: Instrumentalities of the United States organized under an act of Congress (such as Federal Credit Unions).
- 501(c) (2) organizations: Title holding corporations for exempt organizations that collect and pay income from property to exempt organizations.
- 501(c) (4) organizations: Civic leagues, social welfare organizations, local associations of employees.
- 501(c) (5) organizations: Labor, agriculture, and horticultural organizations.
- 501(c) (6) organizations: Business leagues, chambers of commerce, and real estate boards.
- 501(c) (7) organizations: Social and recreational clubs.
- 501(c) (8) organizations: Fraternal beneficiary societies and associations.

- 501(c) (9) organizations: Voluntary employee beneficiary associations.
- 501(c) (10) organizations: Domestic fraternal societies, orders, or associations.
- 501(c) (11) organizations: Teacher's Retirement Funds.
- 501(c) (12) organizations: Local benevolent life insurance associations, mutual ditch or irrigation companies, mutual or cooperative electric or telephone companies and like organizations.
- 501(c) (13) organizations: Cemetery companies.
- 501(c) (14) organizations: State chartered credit unions.
- 501(c) (15) organizations: Small insurance companies and associations providing insurance to members substantially at cost.
- 501(c) (16) organizations: Cooperative organizations to finance crop operations.
- 501(c) (17) organizations: Supplemental unemployment benefit trusts.
- 501(c) (18) organizations: Employee funded pension trusts created before 1959.
- 501(c) (19) organizations: War veterans' organizations.
- 501(c) (20) organizations: Group legal services plan organizations.
- 501(c) (21) organizations: Black lung benefit trusts.
- 501(c) (22) organizations: Withdrawal liability payment funds.
- 501(c) (23) organizations: Veterans' organizations created before 1880.
- 501(c) (25) organizations: Title holding corporations or trusts with multiple parents.
- 501(c) (26) organizations: State sponsored organizations providing health coverage for high-risk individuals.
- 501(c) (27) organizations: State-sponsored Worker's Compensation reinsurance organizations.

- 501(c) (28) organizations: National Railroad Retirement Investment Trusts.
- 501(d) organizations: Religious and apostolic organizations (communal religious communities).
- 501(e) organizations: Cooperative hospital service organizations.
- 501(f) organizations: Cooperative service organizations of operating educational organizations that perform collective investment services for educational organizations.
- 501(k) organizations: Child care organizations.
- 501(n) organizations: Charitable risk pools that pool certain insurance risks of 501(c) (3) organizations.
- 521(a) organizations: Farmers' cooperative organizations.
- 527 organizations: Political organizations accepting contributions or making expenditures for political campaigns.

Now that you know the basic nonprofit categories, let's get you organized with a checklist so you can track your progress as you make it.

CHAPTER 4

DO-IT-YOURSELF CHECKLIST

"Every great dream begins with a dreamer. Always remember, you have within you the strength, the patience, and the passion to reach for the stars to change the world."

—Harriet Tubman

Francis of Assisi said that you eat an elephant one bite at a time, so before you become overwhelmed with the process, just concentrate on taking the bite in front of you, and when you swallow that requirement, go on to the next bite. You will be surprised how quickly you can devour the whole proverbial elephant and form a nonprofit corporation that is state and federally recognized. Each chapter of this book is written in a specific order to help you do the required steps in the right order the first time.

INITIAL SETUP

___Determine the tax-exempt purpose (you can choose more than one)
  ___charitable
  ___religious
  ___educational

WISCONSIN

    ___scientific
    ___literary
    ___testing for public safety
    ___fostering sports competition
    ___preventing cruelty to children
    ___preventing cruelty to animals
___Select business name and make sure it is available
___Is Inc. or Corp. required in business name?
    ___Yes
    ___No
___Get a Federal Employer Identification Number (FEIN)
___Develop a strong mission statement
___Form a board of directors
___*Prepare and file Incorporation
___Complete Compliance requirements
___*Prepare Bylaws
___*Develop Conflict of Interest Policy and Annual Statements
___*Hold and document the first board meeting

*   If you don't want to develop your own Articles of Incorporation, bylaws, conflict of interest documents, and initial organizational meeting minutes from scratch, go to *www.doyourownnonprofit.com* and download the documents and templates to make it fast. The fee for these documents helps fund transportation costs for kids to go to school in Mhlosheni, Swaziland as part of Pasture Valley Children Missions.*

DO YOU QUALIFY FOR FORM 1023-EZ INSTEAD OF FORM 1023?

___ Do You Qualify for the Form 1023-EZ Streamlined Filing? If you answer yes to the next three items, you qualify for the streamlined filing instead of the long filing. You get to skip Chapters 14 – 31 and go straight to Chapter 32.
  ___ Our mission is strictly in the USA with no international involvement or board members.
  ___ Our projected annual budget is under $50,000 a year for the first three years.
  ___ We are not starting a church, school, hospital, or research facility.

COMPLETE IRS FORM 1023 (APPLICATION FOR TAX-EXEMPT STATUS) IF YOU DO NOT QUALIFY FOR FORM 1023-EZ

___ Part I, Identification of Applicant
___ Part II, Organizational Structure
___ Part III, Required Provisions in Your Organizing Document
___ Part IV, Your Activities
___ Part V, Compensation and Other Financial Arrangements
___ Part VI, Financial Data
___ Part VII, Foundation Classification
___ Part VIII, Effective Date
___ Part IX, Annual Filing Requirements
___ Part X, Signature and Upload Checklist

___ Required Schedules (A – H)
  ___ Schedule A: Churches
  ___ Schedule B: Schools, Colleges, and Universities

___Schedule C: Hospitals and Medical
Research Organizations
___Schedule D: Section 509(a) (3) Supporting Organization
___Schedule E: Effective Date
___Schedule F: Low-Income Housing
___Schedule G: Successors to Other Organizations
___Schedule H: Scholarships, Fellowships,
Educational Loans, Or Other Grants

FOLLOW UP TASKS

___Annual Information Tax Return Required by IRS: Form 990, 990-EZ, 990-N, 990-PF
___Submit PS Form 3624, *Application to Mail at Nonprofit Standard Mail Rates*

CHAPTER 5

SELECT A BUSINESS NAME AND MAKE SURE IT IS AVAILABLE

"The difference between the impossible and the possible lies in a man's determination."

—Tommy Lasorda

DESIGNATE ORGANIZATION TYPE AND SUFFIX

Most nonprofits are corporations because that gives the board the most personal protection from lawsuits and other legal matters, and the nonprofit is eligible for more grants than other forms of organization. Some states do not allow you to register other organization types, so corporation is your only choice.

Don't let the designation *corporation* scare you. You can start small and stay small, or start small and grow huge. That depends on what you do to grow the organization. Some states require a designation suffix at the end of the organization name such as *Inc., Corp, Incorporated,* or *Corporation*. Kitty set up Pasture Valley Children Missions in Missouri where no suffix is required, but it is optional. Michigan forbids using a suffix. Florida requires a suffix (even for churches!), so the name would have been Pasture Valley Children Missions, Inc. It just depends on where you live.

> **In Wisconsin, a suffix IS required.**

PICK A GREAT NAME

You must have a unique name, different from all other business and organization names in the state. Also, be careful not to pick something too close to well-known nonprofits, even if they are in other states. Very similar names can cause confusion as well as claims of trademark/service mark infringement from the other corporation. Spend some time thinking about what your organization represents and come up with a name that fits what you plan to do.

When you select a name for your nonprofit, keep it short and explanatory. Leave off words like *charity, organization, nonprofit,* and *foundation* (unless you are a foundation, which is different from a public charity). You might also want to leave off *The* and *A* at the beginning of the organization's name. IRS does not put *The* and *A* in their records, but states do. It could cause donor confusion when they try to check you out if the names do not match between the state and IRS, or they cannot find you in the IRS database. Best to leave *The* and *A* out of the name. In any case, you want the name to fit the mission that is easy to remember and has hearing appeal.

Let us give you some examples of what we mean:

- If you had vision problems, which would you contact first? *Visual Impairment League* or *Modern Vision Clinic*? Most people would contact *Modern Vision Clinic* because it sounds state-of-the-art and is easy to understand.

- If you wanted to get a pet for your kids but didn't want to spend a lot of money, would you select *Storm Cat Rescue* (an actual nonprofit in North Carolina) or *Animal Welfare League of Montgomery County* (an actual nonprofit in Maryland)?
- If you were selecting a Christian daycare center for your toddler, would you pick *The Institute of Divine Developmental and Cognitive Child Care* or *All God's Kids*? Most people would pick *All God's Kids* because it is friendly, short, easy to remember, and makes a statement about how the organization feels about children.
- If you were looking for some help with a legal matter but had limited funds, would you contact *Criminal and Civil Litigation Foundation* or *Legal Aid Services*? If you are like us, you pick the one that isn't a mouthful of gobbledygook.

For Kitty's first organization, she chose *Pasture Valley Children Missions*. We get donation checks in that say *Pasture Valley Children's Mission*. If she had been smart back then, she would have just called it *Pasture Valley Children* because it fits on a check more easily and isn't confusing. She learned her lesson and named the second nonprofit *BenevoLance* (the website for benevolence was already taken, and *Lance* lent itself to an attractive logo that projected taking the Sword of the Lord [the power of Jehovah] to the poor of the world).

People like to keep it simple. Our friend Judy Hanna wrote a book called *Ageism Activism*. It was a wonderful book of resources and information about how to spot elderly and senior abuse and discrimination and what to do about it. The book didn't do well until she changed the name to *Should I Be Afraid?* Then she got lots of readers' attention. The same holds true with your nonprofit. Get lots of attention by picking a clever, catchy, short, and explanatory name. Pick a name that rolls smoothly off the tongue and lends itself to an attractive or memorable logo. Leave off words that add nothing to the meaning and keep it short so it fits on a donation check. When in doubt, explain your nonprofit to 8-year-olds and ask them what you should call it. They will know!

IS THE NAME AVAILABLE?

Next, check with the state's corporation division to find out if the name is available. You can call the state's corporation division, or you can check name availability online by Googling the state combined with "business entity search."

Once you have decided what to call your nonprofit, your next step will be to get a Federal Employer Identification Number. Details follow in the next chapter.

CHAPTER 6

GET A FEDERAL EMPLOYER IDENTIFICATION NUMBER (FEIN)

"What you finish is more important than what you begin."

—MIKE MURDOCK

FEDERAL EMPLOYER IDENTIFICATION NUMBER (FEIN)

The Federal Employer Identification Number (FEIN) is like a social security number for all kinds of businesses, whether for-profit or nonprofit. It is a nine-digit number assigned for tax filing and reporting purposes. The FEIN format is XX – XXXXXXX, different from social security numbers in which the format is XXX – XX – XXXX.

As confusing as it may seem – with the word *employer* in its name – you do not have to employ anyone to need this number. And to be even more confusing, it goes by other names. It is sometimes referred to as

- Employer Identification Number (EIN),
- Tax Identification Number or Tax ID Number (TIN), and

- IRS Form CP 575 E (If you register it correctly, the letter E will be on the end for exempt organizations on the CP 575 confirmation notice)
- SS-4. This is the mail-in or fax-in application to get an EIN. IRS returns the number handwritten on the SS-4, so some people confuse the application with the number and call the FEIN the SS-4.

The FEIN does not designate your organization as tax-exempt. Rather it identifies the organization as an *existing recognized business entity*. You must have the FEIN to open a bank account for your nonprofit organization, and some states require that number to file your articles of organization with the state. Make sure the organization name is the same with IRS as it is with the state, including any suffix (such as Inc. or Corp.) that you included in the name.

Only one FEIN is assigned to an organization, and it never expires, even if not used for a long time. You cannot get a new FEIN for the same organization if you lose the number or forget it. If you lose the number and you have set up a bank account, you can contact the bank, and they can look it up. You can contact IRS by calling the Business and Specialty Tax Line at (800) 829-4933. They will give you the Tax ID number over the phone if you are an authorized person (such as an officer of the organization).

You cannot use an EIN from another business you already have. A nonprofit is a separate entity, and you must register it with IRS separately. You can have a dozen EINs for different businesses, but you still need a new one for the nonprofit.

FEIN is free. IRS does not charge a fee to get this number, but lots of websites want to charge $49 to $79 to get it for you. You can do this yourself in five minutes at no charge.

The words *The* or *A* at the beginning of an organization's name will not show up in the EIN paperwork. Also, the only punctuation and special characters allowed on the EIN application are hyphen (-) and ampersand (&). That means you leave off all commas, periods, etc. For example, IRS would process *The John Smith Evangelical Ministries, Inc.* as *JOHN SMITH EVANGELICAL MINISTRIES INC*

TWO WAYS TO GET AN FEIN NUMBER:

1. THE ONLINE OPTION:

The easiest and fastest way to get an EIN is online between 7 a.m. and 10 p.m. Eastern time Monday through Friday. You get the FEIN in real time. The online option is not available nights, weekends, or holidays. Do an internet search for "FEIN ONLINE" and click on the IRS link. There will be other links that want to charge you; skip them and click on the IRS link. Here is the link you want: *https://www.irs.gov/businesses/small-businesses-self-employed/apply-for-an-employer-identification-number-ein-online* which leads you to this link (you can go directly if you type it in): *https://sa.www4.irs.gov/modiein/individual/index.jsp*

> **NOTE:** You need a social security number to get an Employer Identification Number issued online. If no one on your board has a social, you can use an Individual Taxpayer Identification Number (ITIN) and mail or fax in the request using Form SS-4. For foreign organizations, write *FOREIGN* where it asks for your social security number. If no one on the board has a social or ITIN, someone on the board may want to apply for an ITIN using IRS Form W-7, or you can ask a U. S. citizen to join your board. ITINs take about seven weeks to come back.

Some notes on what to click on using the online FEIN application:

1. Your Type of Legal Structure answer is: *View additional types including Tax-Exempt and Government Organizations.*
2. Additional Types: If you are setting up a church, click on *church*. Otherwise, click on *Other Nonprofit/Tax Exempt Organizations* at the bottom of the screen.
3. Why is the Nonprofit Requesting an EIN? Answer: *Started a new business*
4. Who is the Responsible Party? Answer: *Individual*
5. You will need to put your name and social security number as they appear on your social security card. Anyone on your board of directors can put in their name and social. That is how IRS ensures that a person from the U.S. is applying and not some international terrorist group or something similar trying to funnel money through a nonprofit into illegal activities. Using your social to get a nonprofit EIN does **not** affect your personal income tax return in any way. IRS just needs a warm body with a social to get the EIN online. Once you enter the name and social, click on *I am a responsible and duly authorized member or officer having knowledge of the organization's affairs.* If the responsible party changes over time, you have to notify IRS of the new responsible party on Form 8822-B.
6. When you put in the physical address for the nonprofit (which can be your address at home; you don't need to get a different address), you have the option of adding a mailing address or post office box as well if you prefer to get your mail somewhere else.
7. When you put in the name of the organization, remember to add *Inc* or *Corp* if that is part of your organization name (but leave off the period at the end).
8. 8. On the screen that says *Tell us more about the Nonprofit/Tax-Exempt Organization,* most or all the answers will be

NO. If you click on employees, even though you don't currently have employees, IRS will code your EIN to expect employee withholding reports and payments from you. If you are just starting, you might want to check *NO* for everything. Once you get employees, you can file the necessary reports and submit withholding taxes to IRS.

The next screen will ask you to specify your type of services (retail, insurance, health care, transportation, etc.). Just check *Other* at the bottom. On the next page, choose *Other* again and enter about five words or less to explain your purpose briefly. Some examples that will fit include:

- Tangible assistance to the needy
- Orphan care in Africa
- Job training for veterans
- Assist elderly and handicapped
- Drug prevention and awareness
- After-school childrens programs (no apostrophe in children's, IRS doesn't allow punctuation except for hyphen and ampersand)
- Support system for cancer patients

When asked how you want to receive your EIN, click on **Receive letter online**. The next screen will be a review of all information you submitted. Proofread the name, address, and other information before submitting. If you made a mistake such as forgetting *Inc* or *Corp*, your only choice is to start over. There is a button at the top right of the screen to start a new EIN. That is how you start over before the first EIN is issued in error. If there are no errors, click to submit and your EIN will come up on the screen.

WRITE DOWN THE NUMBER before touching anything else on your computer! It is a nine-digit number that starts with two digits followed by a dash, then seven more digits. Why write it down before touching anything? Sometimes, when you click on the link to give you the letter, the screen blinks and the EIN is gone. If that happens, you have to call IRS at (800) 829-4933 and ask them for the Tax ID number. Sometimes, that means spending over an hour on hold waiting for someone to answer. Best to write it down just in case. Then click to get the letter and save it to your computer. If you do it correctly, it will be Form CP 575 E.

Although uncommon, there are several reasons your EIN might not process online. When that happens, you will get an error code. Here are some common error codes and what they normally mean:

- **Code 101**: Normally means the name or an extremely similar name is already in use in your state. In that case, call IRS (the number will appear on the screen) or call (800) 829-4933 and make sure someone else on the board didn't already get the EIN and forget to tell you, or that you didn't get it earlier and forgot about it because some time has gone by since then.

    If you did the name availability search from the previous chapter and the name was available, then you shouldn't encounter Code 101. However, what sometimes happens is that an organization years ago got an EIN in the same state for the same name, then closed up shop and dissolved with the state, but forgot to tell IRS that they don't exist anymore. In that case, go ahead and file your state incorporation and send IRS a copy of the approval with the mail-in or fax-in EIN request (IRS Form SS-4). IRS will issue an EIN for your organization even though another exists for the same name in the same state at some time in the past. If the state is willing to approve the name,

IRS will also approve it. If all else fails, tweak the name a little and apply with a slightly different name.
- Codes 102, 103, 105, and 108. These codes normally mean the name and social do not match IRS records. Check your social security card or get someone else on the board to apply for the EIN.
- Codes 109, 110, 112, and 113. These codes normally mean technical problems at IRS or too many people applying for EINs at the same time. Try later.
- Code 114 means you already received one EIN that day with that social and you are limited to one per day. Try again tomorrow or get someone else on the board to use their social to apply. If you made a mistake and started over, it could mean that for some reason, IRS processed the first request and the number was issued. In that case, call IRS and ask to be sure.

THE MAIL-IN OR FAX-IN OPTION

If you do not want to or cannot get your EIN online, you can fill out and mail or fax IRS Form SS-4. You can do an internet search for the form and fill it out online (or print and write it in by hand), and mail to:

Internal Revenue Service Center
ATTN: EIN Operation
Cincinnati, Ohio 45999

You can fax the completed form to (855) 641-6935.

If you fax the form, IRS will fax the FEIN back to the fax number you provided on the SS-4. It normally takes 4 – 5 days. If you mail in the form, the EIN will come back in the mail in about 2 – 3 weeks. If you fax in but do not give a fax number to respond, IRS will mail the EIN in 2 – 3 weeks.

> **NOTE:** Lately IRS has missed some faxes requesting EIN numbers. We have had three clients in which we had to call IRS repeatedly to eventually get the EIN. Not sure what happened, but if you do not hear back by fax in a week, call (800) 829-4933 and ask for the status.

SOME TIPS TO MAKE FORM SS-4 (DECEMBER 2019 FORM) EASY:

Item 9a: Check *Other Nonprofit Organization (specify):* _____. On the line, give a brief description of the purpose or write *Public Charity*.

Item 9b: Put in your state even though you may not already be incorporated.

Item 10: Check *Started a new business*.

Item 11: Use today's date or if you are already incorporated, the incorporation date from the state.

Item 12: The normal answer is 12 (which means the twelfth month or December 31) for the end of the fiscal year. Some educational organizations use June 30 or July 31, but then their tax returns are due near Thanksgiving or right before Christmas, and that puts a damper on the holidays to stop and file nonprofit tax returns, even though nonprofits do not owe any taxes. They still have to file.

Item 13: Normally blank.

Item 14: Normally is not checked.

Item 15: N/A

Item 16: Other: Public Charity.

Item 17: Add a *brief* mission, a few words that describe your purpose, but don't make it too narrow in case you decide to expand it later. *Assist the homeless* is preferable to *Give blankets to homeless on nights when temperatures go below 28 degrees*. Why? Because you might want to also give them hot soup or a place to take a shower, and maybe in ten years you will decide to add some job training to help them get off the street.

Item 18: No. The applicant is the nonprofit, not you personally. No matter how many EINs you have, the organization has none, so the answer is *NO*.

WHAT IF YOU MADE A MISTAKE ON THE FEIN?

If you made a mistake on the FEIN, you need to correct it with IRS. For address errors, use *IRS Form 8822-B, Change of Address or Responsible Party – Business*. You also use this form if the responsible party for the organization changes, for example, if the founding person steps off the board and leaves the organization.

If you forgot to add *Inc.* or *Corp.*, or had a typo in spelling, mail or fax a letter to the EIN section at IRS requesting they correct it. There is no standard form, so just send a letter. Give them the information as it appears on the FEIN CP 575 E form (or another form number if you checked the wrong box instead of *Other Nonprofit/Tax-Exempt Organization*), and then give them the corrected information. Here is the address to use for recently issued EINs that need corrections:

Internal Revenue Service
IRS, Stop 6055
Kansas City, MO 64999
Fax Number: 859-669-5760

A letter may look something like this:

Organization Name
Address
City, ST ZIP

Internal Revenue Service
Stop 6055
Kansas City, MO 64999

Fax: (859) 669-5760

RE: Name Change for FEIN _____

Dear Sir/Ma'am,

Due to administrative oversight, we have an inconsistency between our organization name for FEIN and the name we incorporated with in _____. We put "Inc." as a suffix on the state incorporation but did not include it on the FEIN. I am attaching a copy of our incorporation showing the correct name. Please update your records to reflect the correct name of the organization, which is:

[PLACE CORRECT NAME HERE]

Thank you,

Your Name
President (or other office you hold)
Phone Number

IRS will not send a letter acknowledging that they made the change, they will just update your records.

THE CLOCK STARTS TICKING

Once an EIN is issued for a nonprofit, IRS knows your entity exists. Then, when you get incorporated, the clock starts ticking for tax returns. Normally, you incorporate and get the EIN at about the same time. Once you incorporate, you must file a tax return with IRS for the nonprofit *(even if you have no revenues or expenses)* within 4 ½ months of the fiscal year end. For organizations that have December 31 fiscal year end, that means the first nonprofit tax return is due by May 15 of the following year. You do not need 501(c) (3) status to be obligated to file taxes; you just need to be registered with the state as a nonprofit. You file taxes because you are a nonprofit, not because you have 501(c) (3) tax-exempt status with IRS. Either way, you must file an information tax return for the nonprofit every year unless you are a church. Churches are exempt from filing 990-series tax returns.

If there is a time gap between getting the EIN and incorporating with the state, the state effective date will start the clock ticking for tax returns. For example, suppose you got your FEIN in December of one year but did not file the state incorporation until January of the next year. The official start date of the corporation would be January, and that is when the clock started ticking for tax returns. In this example, you would get an extra year before the first tax return is due.

If for some reason you change your mind, or things do not work out, you are not in trouble with IRS if you get the FEIN and never use it. Just let them know you are closing the EIN account.

HOW TO CLOSE AN FEIN ACCOUNT:

If you were issued an FEIN and intended to set up a nonprofit corporation, but you never got around to starting, you can send a letter to IRS asking them to close the FEIN account. You must tell them why, and give them the FEIN number, the legal name of the organization, and the mailing address. If you have a copy of the EIN paperwork, send a copy with the request.

Send to:

>Internal Revenue Service
>Attn: EO Entity
>Mail Stop 6273
>Ogden, UT 84201

>You may fax the request to (855) 214-7520.

You now have several steps out of the way. The next item on your agenda is to create a strong mission statement. More about that in the next chapter.

CHAPTER 7

DEVELOP A STRONG MISSION STATEMENT

"You can only overcome rejection when your goals are more important than approval."

—MIKE MURDOCK

DEFINE THE MISSION YOU ARE ON

Your organization needs a mission statement. If you are the founder(s), you know better than anyone the message you want to convey about your organization. You're on a mission, and your mission statement should reflect your passion. In a sentence or two, what is that mission that motivates you? Your answer should be active, short, inspiring, and cause people to remember you. Erica Olsen said that if your mission statement would make a great t-shirt, it is probably a good one.

LEARN FROM OTHERS

To help you find the right words to express the mission of your organization, we have located a dozen of the best written U. S. nonprofit mission statements for you to study. Notice the statements that get your attention, inspire you, make you want to know more, or match your pre-existing perception of the organization.

> *American Diabetes Association:* To prevent and cure diabetes and to improve the lives of all people affected by diabetes.
> *AmeriCares Foundation*: In times of epic disaster or daily struggle, we deliver medical and humanitarian aid to people in need worldwide.
> *Feed the Children*: Delivers food, medicine, clothing and other necessities to individuals, children and families who lack these essentials due to famine, war, poverty or natural disaster.
> *Good360*: Fulfill the needs of nonprofits with corporate product donations.
> *Habitat for Humanity International*: Seeking to put God's love into action, Habitat for Humanity brings people together to build homes, communities and hope.
> *Humane Society of the United States*: Celebrating Animals, Confronting Cruelty.
> *Leukemia and Lymphoma Society*: Cure leukemia, lymphoma, Hodgkin's disease and myeloma, and improve the quality of life of patients and their families.
> *Make a Wish Foundation of America*: We grant the wishes of children with life-threatening medical conditions to enrich the human experience with hope, strength and joy.
> *National Multiple Sclerosis Society*: We mobilize people and resources to drive research for a cure and to address the challenges of everyone affected by MS.
> *Smile Train*: Provide a child born with a cleft the same opportunities in life as a child born without a cleft.
> *World Wildlife Federation*: Protecting the future of nature.
> *Wycliffe Bible Translators*: To see a Bible translation program in progress in every language still needing one by 2025.

NOW IT'S YOUR TURN

Now it is time to develop your mission statement. Here are some guidelines to add pizzazz:

- Keep it short: 6–15 words are normally sufficient.
- Use active tense: *We feed hungry kids!* is better than *We strive to eliminate hunger in children.*
- Try your mission statement out on others of different ages and get input.
- Avoid jargon and formal language. Make it so clear a child can understand what is exciting about what you do. Jargon and formal language do not convey your enthusiasm. If in doubt, ask a kid.
- Be specific about the population you serve, but do not box yourself in so that you cannot expand your reach later. Chances are you are not going to eradicate AIDS from the planet, but you can provide antiretroviral medication to Ethiopia's poor. You may provide computers to the poor now, but what about the next latest, greatest, better-than-computers invention? You might want to say *technology* instead of *computers,* so you don't limit yourself down the road.
- Do away with theoretical, scholarly, or academic mission statements.
- Stay away from the words *scholarships* and *grants* unless you have specific criteria established, scholarship or grant committees, applications, etc. Many organizations use *scholarships* and *grants* when in fact they are giving financial assistance that has nothing to do with accredited academics (such as college tuition) or competitive grant proposals. If you tell IRS you are giving scholarships or grants, your 501(c)(3) just got more complicated. Careful that your use of these two words is accurate because IRS asks a lot of questions about both.

- Leave out words that water down the effectiveness of your organization.

Here are a few that you should avoid:

Try	Endeavor
Attempt	Strive
Aim	Pursue
Help	Undertake
Influence	

Instead, use powerful words like these:

Prevent	Mobilize
Abolish	Reduce
Confront	Save
Connect	Solve
Eliminate	Transform
Increase	Improve

- Identify the problem you target, and the solution you provide.
- Use clear, concise, brief, and positive terms to paint a picture of the mission you are on.

You can always change or update your mission statement later if necessary. It doesn't have to be perfect or carved in stone. For now, write it and move on. Notice the missions above do not contain the details of how the organization will operate. The day-to-day logistics of operation must be ironed out by the board of directors; the mission is the *end result* you want from the efforts you make and the logistical considerations you tackle.

In the next chapter, you'll learn how to form your board of directors.

CHAPTER 8

FORM A BOARD OF DIRECTORS

"Opportunity is missed by most people because it is dressed in overalls and looks like work."

—Thomas Edison

NOT SHAREHOLDERS, BUT STAKEHOLDERS

The Board of Directors is the governing body of a nonprofit. Every officer of the board is a board director, but not every board director has to be an officer. Boards normally have a president, vice president (can have more than one covering different areas such as communications or programs), secretary, and treasurer as officers, and other board members are simply called board members or board directors (those terms are used interchangeably, but the correct name is board director).

> The Board of Directors is the governing body of a nonprofit.

If you are not on the Board of Directors, you have no authority in guiding the organization. Board members are not the managers; management answers to the board of directors. In profit corporations, board members are responsible to the owners (the stockholders). A nonprofit organization is not owned, so board directors answer to:

- The public
- The government
- Their supporters
- The people the organization serves

For-profit corporations are concerned mostly about the bottom line – the money. However, in a nonprofit atmosphere, board members are not shareholders; they are stakeholders. They have a stake in the success of the nonprofit that has little to do with finance.

QUALIFIED AND WILLING

It is a privilege to be on a nonprofit board of directors, and directors should be selected based on qualifications and willingness to serve. They don't need great business acumen or experience but should have good judgment and common sense. The board should be a mix of visionaries and practical souls so that a balance exists, although harmony may not be a 24/7 accomplishment when you put dreamers and realists together. Board members should be matched to board positions that most effectively utilize their skills and talents.

ACCOUNTANT OR ATTORNEY AS BOARD MEMBER?

There are arguments for and against having an accountant or attorney on the board. If you choose to include either, make sure your motives are not so that you can get free expertise. That is unfair to the board member and to the organization. Better to ask them for pro bono or reduced-price services and select board members who have a heart for the organization's mission.

HOW MANY BOARD MEMBERS?

IRS does not specifically establish a set number of board members, but too few or too unqualified can cause delays and questions during the processing phase of your 501(c) (3) application. Relationships are also an important component of board formation. Relatives (by blood or marriage) should hold less than 50% of the vote on a board of directors for a public charity. Foundations can have all family members, but foundations operate with many more limitations than public charities and have lots more paperwork to do.

As a minimum, three board members who are not related, and if two are related, then four or five board members are needed to pass IRS scrutiny. There is no maximum number of board members. There should be as many as are needed to govern the organization. In addition, IRS monitors whether board members are independent members who do not benefit financially from the organization while making board decisions.

Every state has nonprofit business statutes that spell out the minimum number of directors on the board, and the positions of those directors. None require more than a minimum of three except New Hampshire which requires five.

START SMALL

To meet the requirements of IRS, you need at least three board members. To start with, you might do well to keep the number of board members to a minimum. It takes less initial paperwork, and fewer signatures to get everything up and running. The fewer the board members, the fewer people IRS will have to scrutinize. You can add more board members after starting the organization. You might want to consider having an odd number of board members so that there is no tie when voting.

HOW TO ADD BOARD MEMBERS

You get to pick who is on the initial board. Consider approaching potential board members to be *interim* (temporary) board members until the first election which is normally held at the beginning of a new fiscal year. That way, if they don't work out, they are only in your hair for a short time. To add members later, simply vote in new board members at a board meeting. Document the vote in the board meeting minutes.

HOW TO REMOVE BOARD MEMBERS

When you want to get someone off the board, you can address it with the person one-on-one and ask them to resign. If they refuse, you bring it to a vote at a board meeting, whether a regular meeting or one called specifically to vote on removing the board member. Your bylaws tell what percentage of the board must vote for different areas, and they should tell what the required percentage is to remove a board member with or without cause. Suppose the percentage is 75%. That means that if there are three board members total, and two vote to remove a member, that only equals 67% and is not enough to vote the person off the board if they refuse to go willingly. However, if you have four members on the board and three vote for removal, that is 75% and the person causing the problem is gone. Moral of the story: Be very careful who you put on the board. People who are stubborn, argumentative, arrogant, holier-than-thou, always want to be in charge, always know best, or want everything their way don't belong on your board. Just don't invite them to be part of your board. If you need them to fill a slot to help you get the organization started, make them interim (temporary) board members with the understanding that you only need them to serve on your board until the next election of members and then they are free to go with your thanks and gratitude for their selfless service (easier than trying to get rid of them later and risking hard feelings). Another choice would be to make them a non-voting advisor to the board. That way, you get their expertise when you need it, and don't have to deal with them when you don't.

If a problem develops with a member who is not an *interim* director, add some new people to the board before trying to vote the undesirable person out, so you have a high enough percentage to eliminate them from your board. If the troubling person is an officer such as president, there is a way to lessen their influence. During the annual election, the board might vote in a different member to take that officer position and reduce the troublemaker to a regular board position. That would help get the message across that you want them to go away and might make them mad enough to leave on their own. If they don't, you should know that every board member has one vote regardless of position. The president gets one vote, and a regular board member gets one vote. Each vote has the same weight when tallying up the total vote. To vote a person off the board, that person's vote is not part of the tally.

CONVERSATIONS WITH IRS ABOUT YOU GETTING VOTED OFF THE BOARD

Many clients have asked us how to make sure they never get voted off the board. That is a valid concern. If you are going to put your sweat into building an organization, you don't want to lose it. Nonprofits are not owned, and there is a possibility that you could be voted off the board. As a public charity, you cannot make your position a forever carved-in-stone appointment.

One specific client comes to mind, a religious woman in a male-dominated denomination. She was starting a religious school for children and paid for everything out of her pocket to get it started and did most of the work herself to get it going. Sound familiar? She had legitimate concerns that once it was up and running that the male board members would vote her out. It had happened before in other situations she knew about, and she was just plain worried. So, Kitty posed the question of what to do to IRS on her behalf. The answer made all the sense in the world, and we have used it since.

The IRS agent confirmed that board members are not restricted to the same location as the nonprofit. You can have an organization in one state, and all your board members can be in other states (or other countries if you have an international mission). They can be friends, acquaintances, college roommates, old business contacts, or relatives. You can have family members but stay under 50% total voting power to stay off IRS radar.

Every state allows board meetings held by technology such as Skype, GoToMeeting, Google Hangouts, or conference calls as long as everyone can hear everyone else, and all have the capacity to contribute to the meeting. Not much chance of people in other states (or countries) voting you off the board.

To make sure we were given good counsel, Kitty called IRS back two more times and talked with two other agents who gave her the same answer.

MEMBER TRAITS AND QUALITIES

Regardless of the position held by the board member, there are some defining traits and qualities that are essential to successful governance of a nonprofit organization:

- Ethical behavior and integrity
- No conflicts of interest
- Willingness to speak up and voice an opinion (even if unpopular)
- Inclination to cooperate and compromise when necessary
- Eagerness to invest the time necessary to succeed

Below are basic job descriptions for the most common positions on the Board of Directors. You can tailor the job descriptions to whatever your organization needs from the board members. You can call the positions whatever you want; you are not limited to the titles given.

President (or Chairman) of the Board

Chairman sounds more like a title for a profit corporation, so President is often used for nonprofit corporations. Helpful attributes include:

- Leadership skills
- Earned respect of board members
- Good communication skills
- Ability to make hard calls when difficult decisions must be made
- Willingness to delegate

If you are the founder and you have those qualifications, then consider making yourself the initial President of the Board of Directors. You may be the most qualified person for the job.

A sample job description might be:

The President of the Board represents the organization as ambassador to the community; presides over the affairs of the board and assists in setting agendas for board meetings; coordinates establishment of committees, assignments, and execution of tasks; steers board selection of an Executive Director; leads strategic planning and fundraising efforts; recruits and trains new board members; and delegates responsibility and authority to accomplish the goals of the organization.

Vice President (or Vice Chairman) of the Board

The Vice President is sometimes the successor to the President, a President in Training, or President-elect. The corporate bylaws should reflect whether that is the case. Helpful attributes for Vice President are the same as for the President.

A sample job description might be:

> The Vice President of the Board acts as the President when the President is not available. He or she assists the President in executing duties and performs other duties as assigned by the Board.

Secretary of the Board

The Secretary of the Board is the communication and recordkeeping member of the Board of Directors. He or she should be familiar with the mission and vision of the organization, the Articles of Incorporation, and the bylaws. Helpful attributes include an aptitude for organization, writing abilities, and communication competence.

A sample job description might be:

> The Secretary of the Board maintains records of all Board actions; prepares and distributes meeting minutes; safeguards all corporation records; presides over meetings in the absence of the President and Vice President; and performs other duties as assigned by the Board.

Treasurer (or Chief Financial Officer, CFO) of the Board

The Treasurer or CFO of the Board is the go-to person for financial questions in an organization. He or she must be above reproach with integrity, and maintain transparency in performing the duties of the office. Helpful attributes for Treasurer include critical thinking skills, analytical ability, and willingness to learn financial accounting principles as they relate to nonprofit organizations. The Treasurer does not have to actually prepare financial reports, but must make sure they get done.

A sample job description might be:

> *The Treasurer of the Board coordinates and ensures financial stewardship and financial well-being of the organization; manages finances; ensures timely and accurate filing of financial reports to IRS and state agencies; presents annual budgets for board approval; reviews annual audits; signs and deposits checks; and performs other duties as assigned by the Board.*

Board Member or Board Director

Not every member of the Board of Directors needs to hold a title to an office, but all board officers are directors. In other words, whether a board member holds an office or not, they are still board directors. *Board member* and *board director* mean the same thing, but board director is the correct term; board member is the casual term. All positions are important and add to the effective governance of a nonprofit organization. Each board member should be a volunteer who is committed to the mission of the organization. This is a person who is willing to make time and actively participate in board meetings, fundraising activities, and public events involving the organization. In addition to investing time, board members should also be willing to invest

> **All positions are important and add to the effective governance of a nonprofit organization.**

money. Each member should have a copy of the organization's conflict of interest policy and sign a disclosure form annually.

A sample job description might be:

> *Board Members attend regularly scheduled board meetings; actively participate in decision making, considering the best interest of the organization; maintain integrity in use of resources; adhere to the letter and intent of regulatory guidance; establish and carry out planning, policies, fundraising, and budgeting; and evaluate the Executive Director's (if there is one) performance and compensation annually.*

SHOULD WE HAVE AN EXECUTIVE DIRECTOR?

Most new organizations do not need a paid program director, executive director, or someone with a similar job title. Paid employees work for and report to the Board of Directors. Once the organization grows big enough to need a program director, then is the time to get to work finding the best fit for the position. So, how do you do that?

Start by thinking about what the requirements would be for a paid position to run your program. Have the board members do some research between board meetings. They will need to create the job description, determine the hours, and set the pay based on qualifications needed and the organization's budget. When determining compensation, you need to make sure it is reasonable for the services performed, and comparable to other nonprofits of similar size and mission.

> **Start by thinking about what the requirements would be for a paid position to run your program.**

Once you have some parameters to work within, discuss the details at a board meeting. When the details are ironed out, someone makes a motion to hire a program director (by whatever name you come up with), approve the job description, confirm the hours and pay, and set a start date for the position. Then you begin seeking candidates to fill the position.

If someone on your board turns out to be the best qualified for the job, that is not an issue. As long as the pay is reasonable and the work is actually being performed, go ahead and hire that person. However, board members cannot vote to hire themselves; it is a conflict of interest. Make the person leave the room while the rest of the board votes to hire him or her (even if that turns out to be you, you have to leave the room for the vote). It is acceptable for a board member to also be a paid director, although we don't recommend it until the organization has 501(c)(3) approval (paperwork is simpler if you wait) and is financially able to support the position. If you hire a board member as the program director, that member doesn't get paid to go to board meetings; he or she gets paid to run the organization's programs under board supervision. Also, be aware of the percentages spent on salaries and benefits compared to the overall budget. If the organization takes in $50,000 a year and pays out $40,000 to the program director, that could be a huge red flag at IRS depending on the mission. If the program is an after-school volunteer tutoring program, RED FLAG! If the program is counseling veterans with PTSD and the salaries are for trained psychologists and therapists, then there is no red flag.

With your board of directors now in place, you are ready to learn about incorporation.

> If you hire a board member as the program director, that member doesn't get paid to go to board meetings; he or she gets paid to run the organization's programs under board supervision.

CHAPTER 9

CRASH COURSE ON INCORPORATION

"Nothing will ever be attempted, if all possible objections must first be overcome."

—Samuel Jackson

THE BIRTH OF AN ORGANIZATION

When a child is born, a vital record of that birth is created in the state in which the child was born – it's called the *Birth Certificate*. It's recorded by the state, and it registers the presence of a new little person. The certificate documents who the parents are, where and when the child was born, and other important information verifying the child's existence. The child is given a name, and in some cases, a suffix (such as Jr. or III) that further identifies the child. The child's origin is declared, such as Caucasian, Hispanic, or Native American. The parents complete the paperwork and the hospital sends it to the bureau of vital records (by whatever name the state calls that department), and a birth certificate is created.

When a nonprofit corporation is born, a vital record of that birth is created in the state in which the organization was born – it's normally called the *Articles of Incorporation*. It is recorded by the state, and it registers the presence of a new organization. The paperwork declares who the parents are (the incorporators), where and when the organization was born, and other vital information verifying the organization's existence. The nonprofit is given a name, and in some cases, a suffix (such as Inc. or Corp.) that further identifies the organization. The nonprofit's origin is declared, such as Public Benefit, Mutual Benefit, or Religious. The incorporator completes the paperwork and submits it to the state's Corporations Division, and a *business birth certificate* (figuratively speaking) is created.

A MATTER OF PUBLIC RECORD

A birth certificate is a public record in the sense that if you are related and have a need to know, you can get a copy. The analogy differs when compared to a nonprofit corporation. Incorporation records are public records and as such are available to the public. Anyone wishing access is allowed to see, read, and have a copy of your nonprofit's birth certificate. For this reason, it's a good idea to leave out social security numbers and other personal identifiers in the documents you file.

Public charitable foundations, funds, community chests, and some trusts may also be eligible for 501(c)(3) status under certain circumstances, if they exist for charitable purposes. Their filing requirements are similar to nonprofit corporations, but their documents have different names, such as *Articles of Association* instead of *Articles of Incorporation*. Incorporation provides more legal protection for officers than unincorporated organizations.

TYPES OF NONPROFITS

To establish a vital record with your state and IRS, you must decide the origin or type of organization because it has far-reaching consequences for 501(c)(3) status. There are three broad categories of nonprofits:

Public Benefit

A public benefit organization is normally a charity with a charitable mission, and IRS recognizes this type of organization for 501(c) (3) tax-exempt status. A public benefit corporation cannot be established to help just one organization (such as a specific orphanage) or individual (such as a particular orphan) but must benefit a class of people or group of organizations (such as potentially benefiting any orphan or orphanage in Mexico). You can start small by initially benefiting one or two specific orphanages, but must allow for helping others in the same category or class. If your nonprofit benefits only one organization or a defined finite group of people who can be identified by name (such as a family), it is a private foundation, not a public benefit corporation. This differentiation does not mean that your public charity cannot help an individual or a family, but it does mean that you cannot limit your efforts in establishing a nonprofit to specific people or families, you must leave room to grow and add people or families whose names you do not know yet.

Public benefit organizations handling less than $5,000 per year are automatically exempt and do not need to file for 501(c) (3) tax-exempt status until they reach the $5,000 revenue level in a given fiscal year. Regardless of revenues, *all* nonprofits except churches must file annual nonprofit tax returns, even if they have no income or expenses.

Feed the Children and *United Way* are examples of Public Benefit nonprofits.

Mutual Benefit

A mutual benefit nonprofit exists to benefit members of a group. It is similar to a club. People pay membership fees or join the group, and assets are distributed among the members if the organization dissolves. IRS does not normally give 501(c) (3) status to mutual benefit organizations because they serve their members, not the public. Examples are an electric cooperative association or the local chapter of the *Veterans of Foreign Wars*. They are nonprofits, but not 501(c)(3) tax-exempt nonprofits.

Religious

There are two kinds of religious nonprofits: denominational churches and other religious organizations.

Denominational churches never have to file for 501(c)(3) tax-exempt status because they are automatically exempt, and donations are automatically deductible. However, once a church gets twenty-five or more members (not attendees, actual members who have met the membership requirements and been accepted as church members), they normally apply for 501(c)(3) status to soothe the anxieties of their tithers who worry that IRS might turn down their tax deductions. When that time arrives, denominational churches must jump through a lot of hoops to get church status, but it is worth the effort because once church status is granted, the church never has to file tax returns and the congregation can rest assured that their tithes and offerings are tax deductible. IRS can audit a church based on complaints, but other than that, IRS has little to do with approved churches once they give the stamp of approval. That may be why IRS makes churches answer to fourteen extra requirements that other nonprofits do not have.

Nondenominational churches, evangelical ministries, and other religious nonprofits are eligible for 501(c)(3) status from IRS, but they must file tax returns every year.

Samaritan's Purse is an example of a religious nonprofit, and *World Vision* is an example of a church (yes, they started as a church).

FOREIGN VS. DOMESTIC CORPORATION

To conduct nonprofit business in more than one state, you must first be recognized as a nonprofit entity in your own state by filing an incorporation document such as *Articles of Incorporation*, which gets you a business birth certificate, figuratively speaking. Then you can apply to the Corporations Division in other states as a *foreign* nonprofit corporation for recognition and approval to conduct nonprofit business in their state as well. The application you complete asking permission to operate in another state results in a *Certificate of Authority* from the other state saying you can do business in their state, too. You are not incorporating in other state, you only have one business birth certificate, but you can operate in the other state with the permission granted by getting approved for a Certificate of Authority.

Foreign does not mean foreign country, it means from outside the state boundaries; *domestic* means inside the state boundaries. You are a domestic corporation in the state where you incorporate, and a foreign corporation in all other states. It normally costs more to be registered as a foreign nonprofit corporation than a domestic nonprofit in a state. Outsiders usually get charged more.

Each state has its own requirements, fees, and forms for Certificate of Authority. Most states require proof that you are approved, and that your organization is doing reputable business in your home state. This requirement is usually met by providing a recently certified copy of your state's *Certificate of Good Standing*, *Certificate of Existence*, *Certificate of Fact* (Texas), or similar state document. It is a piece of paper provided by your Corporations Division that you pay to have certified, usually not more than 60 days prior to applying to another state for approval to conduct business. If the good standing paperwork gets too old, you have to pay to get another copy certified with a more recent date.

Getting a Certificate of Authority to operate in a state is not the same thing as being approved to do fundraising in that state. Those are two separate functions. Thirty-eight states and District of Columbia have charitable registration. You pay a fee, file a form, provide requested copies of documents, and you are allowed to raise funds once approved, except in Illinois. They run twelve to eighteen months behind on processing charitable registration (we are not making it up!), so you can start raising funds in good faith as soon as you mail the registration to Illinois. Send it with tracking, so you have proof of the date you sent it.

WHAT IF I MOVE OFTEN? WHAT HAPPENS TO THE NONPROFIT?

Pick the state to incorporate in carefully. If you move around a lot, Delaware is friendly to nonprofits and is a good choice. Delaware does not have charitable registration, so that is a plus. Many corporations register in Delaware and operate elsewhere because it is easy to get registered and stay compliant without a bunch of ongoing paperwork like California has. You can register in Delaware and get a Certificate of Authority for the state you live in. Then when you move, get a Certificate of Authority for the new state, and your 501(c)(3) remains in force. You can actually do that in any state, but Delaware is often picked as the home state because it has good laws to attract businesses.

NEW: REVENUE PROCEDURE 2018-15

IRS made a change to their policy when they published Revenue Procedure 2018-15. Before this change, you could not permanently move your tax-exempt organization to another state without filing for a new 501(c)(3). You had to start from scratch in the new state. However, with Revenue Procedure 2018-15, you can move from state to state and take your 501(c)(3) with you. If states allow domestication, you file domestication paperwork with both states (the one you are leaving and the one you are moving to). If not, you file incorporation in the new state, and close the organization in the original state. Be sure to notify IRS of the address change on Form 8822-B and on the annual tax return. There is no fee to IRS for moving your 501(c)(3) to another state. You have to pay the domestication, dissolution, and/or incorporation fees to the states, but nothing to IRS.

REQUIREMENT FOR REGISTERED AGENT

To do business as either a domestic or a foreign nonprofit corporation, you must have a *registered agent*. This is a person or business in the state where you want to conduct business who agrees to be the eyes and ears for the nonprofit. The registered agent's purpose is to give the Corporations Division a contact person with a street address (as opposed to a post office box) inside the state lines who will receive official mail, handle complaints, answer telephone inquiries from state offices, and just generally be the go-to person or company on behalf of your nonprofit. Don't worry, if the state asks a question the registered agent cannot answer, they have time to contact you and get the answer.

You can be the registered agent for your organization in your state if you are willing to be the face and voice behind the corporate name and mission. The registered agent can be a commercial agent or a non-commercial agent. It can be an individual or organization willing to be your representative, or it can be a company for hire who is licensed by the state to represent other organizations.

To find a commercial registered agent, you can do an internet search for registered agent and the state, or you can call the Corporation Division and ask for a list of approved registered agents in the state. If you get Certificates of Authority to operate in all 50 states, you must have registered agents in all those states. Hopefully, you will have friends or family in many of the states who are willing to be your registered agents, so you don't have to hire so many commercial registered agents and pay them every year.

REQUIRED STATEMENTS FOR IRS 501(C) (3) APPROVAL

The exact wording of your incorporation document is not critical except for a few required statements that if missing, will cause your application for 501(c)(3) status to be rejected. If IRS *suggests* something, it is a good idea to follow the suggestion. Here is the IRS *suggested* wording to meet their required language and statements:

Benefit Statement (IRS will not turn down your incorporation if you don't include this, but they suggest that you include these words):

> *No part of the net earnings of the corporation shall inure to the benefit, or be distributable to its members, trustees, officers, or other private persons, except that the corporation shall be authorized and empowered to pay reasonable compensation for services rendered and to make payments and distributions in furtherance of its tax-exempt purposes.*
>
> *No substantial part of the activities of the corporation shall be the carrying on of propaganda, or otherwise attempting to influence legislation, and the corporation shall not participate in, or intervene in (including the publishing or distribution of statements) any political campaign on behalf of or in opposition to any candidate for public office.*
>
> *Notwithstanding any other provision of these articles, the corporation shall not carry on any other activities not permitted to be carried on (a) by a corporation exempt from federal income tax under Section 501(c)(3) of the Internal Revenue Code, or the corresponding section of any future*

federal tax code, or (b) by a corporation, contributions to which are deductible under Section 170(c) (2) of the Internal Revenue Code, or the corresponding section of any future federal tax code.

Purpose Statement (IRS will turn down your incorporation without this statement):

Said Corporation is organized exclusively for charitable, religious, educational, and scientific purposes, including, for such purposes, the making of distributions to organizations that qualify as exempt organizations under Section 501(c) (3) of the Internal Revenue Code, or the corresponding section of any future federal tax code.

If you have an objection to religious or scientific purposes, you can leave those out if desired.

Dissolution Statement (IRS will turn down your incorporation without the first sentence, but suggest you include the second sentence as well, even though it sounds like a bunch of legal mumbo-jumbo):

Upon the dissolution of the corporation, assets shall be distributed for one or more exempt purposes within the meaning of Section 501(c) (3) of the Internal Revenue Code, or corresponding section of any future federal tax code, or shall be distributed to the federal government, or to a state or local government, for a public purpose. Any such assets not so disposed of shall be disposed of by a Court of Competent Jurisdiction of the county in which the principal office of the corporation is then located, exclusively for such purposes or to such organization or organizations as said Court shall determine which are organized and operated exclusively for such purposes.

WISCONSIN

REQUIRED WORDING FOR FOUNDATIONS:

If you are an actual foundation (not a public charity with the word *Foundation* in the organization name), you need to either rely on state law for foundation rules (if your state allows it – see Appendix B for list of states and rules), or you need to put this in your incorporation paperwork:

> *As a private foundation, we meet IRS requirement for foundations in addition to 501(c) (3) requirements as follows:*
>
> 1. *The corporation will distribute its income for each tax year at a time and in a manner as not to become subject to the tax on undistributed income imposed by section 4942 of the Internal Revenue Code, or the corresponding section of any future federal tax code.*
> 2. *The corporation won't engage in any act of self-dealing as defined in section 4941(d) of the Internal Revenue Code, or the corresponding section of any future federal tax code.*
> 3. *The corporation won't retain any excess business holdings as defined in section 4943(c) of the Internal Revenue Code, or the corresponding section of any future federal tax code.*
> 4. *The corporation won't make any investments in a manner as to subject it to tax under section 4944 of the Internal Revenue Code, or the corresponding section of any future federal tax code.*
> 5. *The corporation won't make any taxable expenditures as defined in section 4945(d) of the Internal Revenue Code, or the corresponding section of any future federal tax code.*

If you are foundation, if you are not sure whether you can rely on state law for foundation requirements, add the above to your articles. If you are not a foundation, but are instead a public charity, do not include the information above or change it instead to read (this is **optional for public charities**):

In any year we are classified as a private foundation, we meet IRS requirement for foundations in addition to 501c3 requirements as follows:

1. *The corporation will distribute its income for each tax year at a time and in a manner as not to become subject to the tax on undistributed income imposed by section 4942 of the Internal Revenue Code, or the corresponding section of any future federal tax code.*
2. *The corporation won't engage in any act of self-dealing as defined in section 4941(d) of the Internal Revenue Code, or the corresponding section of any future federal tax code.*
3. *The corporation won't retain any excess business holdings as defined in section 4943(c) of the Internal Revenue Code, or the corresponding section of any future federal tax code.*
4. *The corporation won't make any investments in a manner as to subject it to tax under section 4944 of the Internal Revenue Code, or the corresponding section of any future federal tax code.*
5. *The corporation won't make any taxable expenditures as defined in section 4945(d) of the Internal Revenue Code, or the corresponding section of any future federal tax code.*

INFORMATION FOR INCORPORATION

There is some relatively constant information across states that should be included in the incorporation document. Every state requires some form of the following:

- Name of the corporation
- Type of corporation: public benefit, mutual benefit, or religious
- Duration (normally perpetual)
- Street address and mailing address of the initial registered office and the name of the initial registered agent
- The name of the incorporator(s)
- The purpose and dissolution statements (and foundation statement for actual foundations). These statements are not required by the state but required by IRS. You can also include the benefit statement suggested by IRS.
- Whether the corporation has members. Most nonprofits DO NOT have members. Organizations are either run by the Board of Directors or by the membership. The question about members means membership. Being run by a Board of Directors is a directorship, not a membership. It is normally an either/or choice.
- Who will manage the affairs of the corporation? (normally the Board of Directors)
- The number of directors (make sure you include the required positions for your state)
- The term and manner of election of directors (you can say that they will be as provided or described in the Bylaws)
- That the Articles can be amended by the Board of Directors in the manner provided by the Bylaws (unless you want to include those details in the incorporation documents)
- Articles to protect directors and officers from lawsuits (optional)

- A statement that the corporation may purchase general comprehensive liability insurance covering the board members and officers in the performance of their duties (optional)
- An affirmation that all information is true and correct, and execution by signature(s) by the incorporator(s) on a specific date

Now that you know bits and pieces about incorporation, let's get your nonprofit incorporation paperwork done.

CHAPTER 10

LET'S INCORPORATE AND STAY COMPLIANT!

*It's One Thing to Talk About What is Wrong -
It's Another to Actually Do Something About It.*

—STEVE WOOD, NEW BRAUNFELS, TEXAS

In addition to IRS codes, every state has nonprofit business statutes that spell out the minimum number of directors on the board, and the positions of those directors. Wisconsin allows one person to hold more than one office at a time. Below are your statute and board composition guidelines:

- Statute: Wisconsin Annotated Code, Chapter 181, Nonstock Corporations
- Minimum Board Members: 3
- Required Offices: President, Secretary, Treasurer

*If you start with 3 members, you might have President, Vice President, and one person can be Secretary and Treasurer simultaneously, but you still need at least three board members minimum counting the officers.

WHAT YOU DO TO GET INCORPORATED

Wisconsin offers online filing but does not provide space or a place to include the IRS-required 501(c) (3) clauses, so DO NOT use the online option.

Instead you will file the paper Form 102 *Nonstock Corporation Articles of Incorporation*. You can get a copy of it at *https://www.wdfi.org/_resources/indexed/site/corporations/dfi-corp-102.pdf*

The form is straightforward, but also does not include the 501(c)(3) language, so you will need to type up the template below to create an attachment containing the IRS required clauses.

> *Note: If you do not want to type this template, you can get it at www.doyourownnonprofit.org under the State Templates tab as a single item or as part of a package of nonprofit documents ready to personalize to save time and effort. There is a small charge. Proceeds go to Pasture Valley Children Missions.*

ATTACHMENT TO NONSTOCK ARTICLES OF INCORPORATION

Other Provisions and Purpose Statement:

Benefit Statement: No part of the net earnings of the corporation shall inure to the benefit, or be distributable to its members, trustees, officers, or other private persons, except that the corporation shall be authorized and empowered to pay reasonable compensation for services rendered and to make payments and distributions in furtherance of the purposes set forth in previous articles hereof. No substantial part of the activities of the corporation shall be the carrying on of propaganda, or otherwise attempting to influence legislation, and the corporation shall not participate in, or intervene in (including the publishing or distribution of statements) any political campaign on behalf or in opposition to any candidate for public office. Notwithstanding any other provision of these articles, the corporation shall not carry on any other activities not permitted to be carried on (a) by a corporation exempt from federal income tax under Section 501(c) (3) of the Internal Revenue Code, or the corresponding section of any future federal tax code, or (b) by a corporation, contributions to which are deductible under Section 170(c) (2) of the Internal Revenue Code, or the corresponding section of any future federal tax code.

Purpose Statement: Said Corporation is a church and is organized exclusively for charitable, religious, educational, and scientific purposes, including, for such purposes, the making of distributions to organizations that qualify as exempt organizations under Section 501(c) (3) of the Internal Revenue Code, or the corresponding section of any future federal tax code.

Dissolution Statement: Upon the dissolution of the corporation, assets shall be distributed for one or more exempt purposes within the meaning of Section 501(c) (3) of the Internal Revenue Code, or corresponding section of any future federal tax code, or shall be distributed to the federal government, or to a state or local government, for a public purpose. Any such assets not so disposed of shall be disposed of by a Court of Competent Jurisdiction of the county in which the principal office of the corporation is then located, exclusively for such purposes or to such organization or organizations as said Court shall determine which are organized and operated exclusively for such purposes.

Board Members:

[List Board Members and Addresses]

Submit one signed original and attachment and one copy. A filed copy will be returned to you in one to two weeks. The filing fee is $35 payable to the *Department of Financial Institutions*. You can expedite the filing for an additional $25, but Wisconsin works pretty fast without expediting.
Mail to:

>State of Wisconsin Dept of Financial Institutions \PO Box 93348
>Milwaukee, WI 53293
>Phone: (608) 261-7577

ANNUAL REPORT

The registered agent will get a notice of annual report postcard when it is time to file. It can also be filed online using the printed ID number on the postcard. The annual report has a strange due date: by the anniversary of the end of the quarter in which the organization was incorporated. For example, if your organization incorporated in October of one year, the end of the quarter would be December 31, so the annual report would be due by December 31 of the next year, and by December 31 every year thereafter.

Incorporation Month	Annual Report Due Date
January, February, March	March 31
April, May, June	June 30
July, August, September	September 30
October, November, December	December 31

Filing fee is $10 whether filed by mail or online.

CHARITABLE EXEMPTION

Charities must register for permission to raise funds, but some organizations are exempt from registration. Churches and organizations having under $25,000 revenues with no paid employees, and a few other categories are eligible for charitable exemption. You can review the exemption categories at *https://www.wdfi.org/CharitableOrganizations/faq.htm#COR_exempt* to see if you are eligible, or you can call the charitable registration folks at (608) 267-1711 and ask.

INITIAL CHARITABLE REGISTRATION

If you do not qualify for exemption, before you do any fundraising, you must file initial charitable registration with the state.

You file Form 296 *Charitable Organization Application* located at *https://www.wdfi.org/CharitableOrganizations/forms/dfi-dccs-296.pdf*

This form is long and requires many attachments and must be notarized, so take your time and ask questions if you need help. The number to call is (608) 267-1711. You can also email at *DFICharitableOrgs@wi.gov*

The filing fee for the initial charitable registration is $15 payable to *WDFI*.

Mail application and all required attachments to:

Department of Financial Institutions
Division of Corporate and Consumer Services
PO Box 7879
Madison, Wisconsin 53707-7879

CHARITABLE REGISTRATION RENEWAL

Charitable Registration renewal is done online only in Wisconsin. Renewals are due by July 31, but the state leaves the window to file open between June 1 and September 30 for most organizations. The state sends you an email with a link to click to file the renewal. If you don't want to click the link, you can go to the state website and login. Renewal costs $54 and if you file more than 60 days after the expiration (after September 30), you have to start all over with the initial registration package and send all those attachments again through the mail. Probably best to file on time, easier that way.

SALES TAX EXEMPTION

Nonprofits can get Sales Tax Exemption by filing Form S-103 *Application for Wisconsin Sales and Use Tax Certificate of Exempt Status (CES)*. The form is located at *https://www.revenue.wi.gov/DORForms/s-103.pdf*

Complete the form, assemble the requested attachments, and mail to:

Wisconsin Department of Revenue
PO Box 8902
Madison WI 53708-8902
Phone (608) 266-2776 FAX (608) 267-1030
E-mail: *sales10@revenue.wi.gov*
Website: *www.revenue.wi.gov*

STATE TAX EXEMPTION

Once you receive 501(c) (3) tax-exempt status from IRS, your organization is automatically exempt from state tax in Wisconsin.

CHAPTER 11

LET'S CREATE BYLAWS

"A goal is a dream with a deadline."
—Napoleon Hill

STANDARD OPERATING PROCEDURES

Have you ever been around someone who was or is in the military? They have a language all their own. One of the things they often say is, "It's S-O-P." What they mean is that it is *standard operating procedure*. In Kitty's ten years in the United States Air Force, there were SOPs for everything, normally in the form of regulations, manuals, and technical orders. There was written guidance that addressed just about every foreseeable event or circumstance.

If you look at the nonprofit you are creating as its own army to do good things in the world then you will see the need for SOPs to make your operation as efficient as an Army or Marine rifle platoon. Because you are the incorporator, you may be filling the shoes right now of the Platoon Leader (President), Platoon Sergeant (Vice President), Company Clerk (Secretary), or Quartermaster (Treasurer). People have to know the rules and what is expected so that they can follow them. Your nonprofit corporation's bylaws establish the rules or SOPs in which business is conducted.

CREATING THE CONSTITUTION

Another way to understand the significance of bylaws is to think of them as the organization's constitution. You cannot put everything in the Constitution, only the really important stuff. Once written and approved, it's the way things are done. If you ever want to change something, you have to amend the bylaws, just as you would have to amend the Constitution. Keep trivial aspects that are subject to change (such as the day of the week board meetings are held) out of the bylaws. Be sure to attach any changes to the bylaws directly to the master copy as soon as changes are made.

> You cannot put everything in the Constitution, only the really important stuff.

It is common to make a change, put it in the meeting minutes, but then forget which meeting the change was made, and never attach the change to the master copy of the bylaws. The solution is to assign the responsibility to update the bylaws to one of the board positions. If you keep it simple, there will not be many changes to keep up with.

BYLAW CONTENTS

So exactly what do you put in the bylaws? It depends on which state you live in, but there are some general items addressed in virtually all nonprofit bylaws:

- Name of the organization and the mission.
- How many board members (must meet the minimum established by the state) and what constitutes a quorum. (Normally a majority of members need to be present.)
- Qualifications of board members.

- How officers and board members will be elected and how long they will serve. If you want them to be able to serve more than one term, you need to say so in the bylaws. Also, address limitations on personal liability and the procedures for removing a board member if necessary.
- Duties of Board Members.
- Procedures for calling and conducting meetings, including special and emergency board meetings; and when regular meetings will be held (suggest monthly, bi-monthly, or quarterly, nothing more specific so that you have the flexibility to make changes). In this era of electronics, will you allow board meetings by email, teleconferencing, and/or electronic conferencing software such as Skype? All states allow meetings to take place using technology as long as everyone can hear everyone else, and each can communicate with the rest of the board members.
- How will conflicts of interest be handled? We suggest you reference a conflict of interest policy so that if you ever change procedures, you can more easily update a conflict of interest policy than making formal changes to bylaws.
- How funds will be accounted for and disbursed.
- If the nonprofit has members, what are the classes and rights of membership? (Most 501(c)(3) nonprofits do not have members).
- How committees can be convened and dissolved.
- How bylaws can be changed (for example, by majority vote of the board).
- Accounting or fiscal year that fits the normal flow of activities. Education related activities might need a different fiscal year than an animal shelter. December 31 is the most common fiscal year end.
- Authorize bank signatories by position (such as treasurer and president can sign checks).

WISCONSIN

The following pages include a template for nonprofit bylaws drawn up by an attorney so that you know it contains legal integrity and everything you need to be compliant with the state and IRS. You can delete or modify anything that does not apply to your organization or anything you would rather do differently, but you might be hard pressed to find anything to add. The attorney who created this document was very thorough.

Here are a few things to be aware of in this template:

- 2.03 Nonprofit Status and Exempt Activities Limitation. This section says that you are already approved for 501(c) (3) status. We have it from the attorney's lips that "It is standard practice" to include this clause now so that you do not have to amend the Bylaws later (per Steve Eggleston, J.D.).
- 4.01 Number of Directors. Have at least three board members (five in New Hampshire) as a minimum. Be sure to cover the required officer positions. You can change to another number of board members to fit your board needs as long as you have the minimum. Only the offices required by the state must be filled. For example, many states do not require a Vice President. In that case, you do not have to fill the position of Vice President, but can leave it in the bylaws so it will be easy to add a Vice President down the road if you find that you need one.
- 4.08 Manner of Acting. Paragraph (d) allows meetings to take place by means of modern technology, so everyone does not have to be physically present to be considered in attendance. The entire meeting can be by telephone!
- 5.3 Informal Action by The Board of Directors. This section gives the Board the right to give consent without a meeting, allowing email to be used when a meeting is not needed.
- 8.02 Fiscal Year. The fiscal year is January 1 – December 31. You can change the date if your organization needs a different fiscal year.

If you don't want to type out this template, it is available as a download for a small fee at www.doyourownnonprofit.org (all proceeds go to Pasture Valley Children Missions)

[NAME OF CORPORATION]

NONPROFIT CORPORATE BYLAWS

ARTICLE I
NAME

1.01 Name

The name of this corporation shall be [insert the legal name of your nonprofit].

[Example: The name of this corporation shall be Transcontinental Humanitarian Corp.]

ARTICLE II
PURPOSES AND POWERS

2.01 Purpose

[Insert the legal name of your nonprofit] – hereafter referred to as "The Corporation" is a nonprofit corporation and shall be operated exclusively for charitable, religious, educational, and scientific purposes, including, for such purposes, the making of distributions to organizations that qualify as exempt organizations, under Section 501 (c) (3) of the Internal Revenue Code, or the corresponding section of any future federal tax code.

The Corporation's purpose is to [insert description of specific purpose].

> [Example: The Corporation's purpose is to address, educate, coordinate, and provide aid and relief to eradicate chronic malnutrition and hunger on a local and global level.]

To maximize our impact on current efforts, we may seek to collaborate with other nonprofit organizations which fall under the 501(c) (3) section of the Internal Revenue Code and are operated exclusively for charitable, religious, educational, and scientific purposes.

2.02 Powers

The Corporation shall have the power, directly or indirectly, alone or in conjunction or cooperation with others, to do any and all lawful acts which may be necessary or convenient to affect the charitable purposes, for which The Corporation is organized, and to aid or assist other organizations or persons whose activities further accomplish, foster, or attain such purposes. The powers of The Corporation may include, but not be limited to, the acceptance of contributions from the public and private sectors, whether financial or in-kind contributions.

2.03 Nonprofit Status and Exempt Activities Limitation.

a. Nonprofit Legal Status. The Corporation is a nonprofit corporation, recognized as tax-exempt under Section 501(c)(3) of the United States Internal Revenue Code.
b. Exempt Activities Limitation. Notwithstanding any other provision of these Bylaws, no Director, officer, employee, member, or representative of this corporation shall take any action or carry on any activity by or on behalf of The Corporation not permitted to be taken or carried on by an organization exempt under Section 501(c)(3) of the Internal Revenue Code as it now exists or may be amended, or by any organization contributions to which are deductible under Section 170(c)(2) of such Code and Regulations as it now exists or may be amended. No part of the net earnings of The Corporation shall inure to the benefit or be distributable to any Director, officer, member, or other private person, except that The Corporation shall be authorized and empowered to pay reasonable compensation for services rendered and to make payments and distributions in furtherance of the purposes set forth in the Articles of Incorporation and these Bylaws.
c. Distribution Upon Dissolution. Upon the dissolution of the corporation, assets shall be distributed for one or more exempt purposes within the meaning of Section 501(c)(3) of the Internal Revenue Code, or corresponding section of any future federal tax code, or shall be distributed to the federal government, or to a state or local government, for a public purpose. Any such assets not so disposed of shall be disposed of by a Court of Competent Jurisdiction of the county in which the principal office of the corporation is then located, exclusively for such purposes or to such organization or organizations as said Court shall determine which are organized and operated exclusively for such purposes.

ARTICLE III
MEMBERSHIP

3.01 No Membership Classes

The Corporation shall have no members who have any right to vote or title or interest in or to The Corporation or its properties.

ARTICLE IV
BOARD OF DIRECTORS

4.01 Number of Directors

The Corporation shall have a Board of Directors consisting of at least 3 and no more than 15 Directors. Within these limits, the Board may increase or decrease the number of Directors serving on the Board, including for the purpose of staggering the terms of Directors.

4.02 Powers

All corporate powers shall be exercised by or under the authority of the Board and the affairs of The Corporation shall be managed under the direction of the Board, except as otherwise provided by law.

4.03 Terms

a. All Directors shall be elected to serve a two-year term; however, the term may be extended until a successor has been elected.
b. Director terms shall be staggered so that approximately half the number of Directors will end their terms in any given year.
c. Directors may serve terms in succession.

d. The term of office shall be considered to begin the first month of the fiscal year and end the last day of the second fiscal year in office, unless the term is extended until such time as a successor has been elected.

4.04 Qualifications and Election of Directors

In order to be eligible to serve as a Director on the Board of Directors, the individual must be of legal age sufficient to satisfy state requirements. Directors may be elected at any Board meeting by the majority vote of the existing Board of Directors. The election of Directors to replace those who have fulfilled their term of office shall take place during the first month of each new fiscal year.

4.05 Vacancies

The Board of Directors may fill vacancies due to the expiration of a Director's term of office, resignation, death, or removal of a Director or may appoint new Directors to fill a previously unfilled Board position, subject to the maximum number of Directors under these Bylaws.

> *Unexpected Vacancies.* Vacancies in the Board of Directors due to resignation, death, or removal shall be filled by the Board for the balance of the term of the Director being replaced.

4.06 Removal of Directors

A Director may be removed by [insert your choice of "a majority" or "two-thirds" or "three-fourths"] vote of the Board of Directors then in office, if:

> a. the Director is absent and unexcused from two or more meetings of the Board of Directors in a twelve-month period. The Board President is empowered to excuse

Directors from attendance for reasons deemed adequate by the Board President. The President shall not have the power to excuse him/herself from the Board meeting attendance, and in that case, the Board Vice President shall excuse the President. Or:
b. for cause or no cause, if before any meeting of the Board at which a vote on removal will be made, the Director in question is given electronic or written notification of the Board's intention to discuss her/his case and is given the opportunity to be heard at a meeting of the Board.

4.07 Board of Directors Meetings

Regular Meetings. The Board of Directors shall have a minimum of [Insert the minimum number of regular board meetings you will have] regular meetings each calendar year at times and places fixed by the Board. Board meetings shall be held upon four (4) days' notice by first-class mail, electronic mail, or facsimile transmission or forty-eight (48) hours' notice delivered personally or by telephone. If sent by mail, facsimile transmission, or electronic mail, the notice shall be deemed to be delivered upon its deposit in the mail or transmission system. Notice of meetings shall specify the place, day, and hour of meeting. The purpose of the meeting need not be specified.

Special Meetings. Special meetings of the Board may be called by the President, Vice President, Secretary, Treasurer, or any two (2) other Directors of the Board of Directors. A special meeting must be preceded by at least 2-days' notice to each Director of the date, time, and place, but not the purpose, of the meeting.

Waiver of Notice. Any Director may waive notice of any meeting.

4.08 Manner of Acting.

Quorum. A majority of the Directors in office immediately before a meeting shall constitute a quorum for the transaction of business at that meeting of the Board. No business shall be considered by the Board at any meeting at which a quorum is not present.

Majority Vote. Except as otherwise required by law or by the Articles of Incorporation, the act of the majority of the Directors present at a meeting at which a quorum is present shall be the act of the Board.

Hung Board Decisions. On the occasion that Directors of the Board are unable to make a decision based on a tied number of votes, the President or Treasurer in the order of presence shall have the power to swing the vote based on his/her discretion.

Participation. Except as required otherwise by law, the Articles of Incorporation, or these Bylaws, Directors may participate in a regular or special meeting through the use of any means of communication by which all Directors participating may simultaneously hear each other during the meeting, including in person, internet video meeting or by telephonic conference call.

4.09 Compensation for Board Service

Directors shall receive no compensation for carrying out their duties as Directors. The Board may adopt policies providing for reasonable reimbursement of Directors for expenses incurred in conjunction with carrying out Board responsibilities, such as travel expenses to attend Board meetings.

4.10 Compensation for Professional Services by Directors

Directors are not restricted from being remunerated for professional services provided to The Corporation. Such remuneration shall be reasonable and fair to The Corporation and must be reviewed and approved in accordance with the Board Conflict of Interest Policy and applicable state law.

ARTICLE V
INFORMAL ACTION BY THE BOARD OF DIRECTORS

5.1 Informal Action by The Board of Directors

Any action required or permitted to be taken by the Board of Directors at a meeting may be taken without a meeting if consent in writing, setting forth the action so taken, shall be agreed by the consensus of a quorum. For purposes of this section, an email transmission from an email address on record constitutes a valid writing. The intent of this provision is to allow the Board of Directors to use email to approve actions, as long as a quorum of Board members gives consent.

ARTICLE VI
OFFICERS

6.01 Board Officers

The officers of The Corporation shall be a Board President, Vice President, Secretary, and Treasurer, all of whom shall be chosen by, and serve at the pleasure of, the Board of Directors. Each Board officer shall have the authority and shall perform the duties set forth in these Bylaws or by resolution of the Board or by direction of an officer authorized by the Board to prescribe the duties and authority of other officers. The Board may also appoint additional Vice Presidents and such other officers as it deems expedient for the proper conduct of the business of The Corporation, each of whom shall have such authority and shall perform such duties as the Board of Directors may determine. No Board officer may act

> No Board officer may act in more than one capacity where action of two or more officers is required.

in more than one capacity where action of two or more officers is required.

6.02 Term of Office

Each officer shall serve a two-year term of office and may serve consecutive terms of office.

6.03 Removal and Resignation

The Board of Directors may remove an officer at any time, with or without cause. Any officer may resign at any time by giving written notice to The Corporation without prejudice to the rights, if any, of The Corporation under any contract to which the officer is a party. Any resignation shall take effect at the date of the receipt of the notice or at any later time specified in the notice unless otherwise specified in the notice. The acceptance of the resignation shall not be necessary to make it effective.

6.04 Board President

The Board President shall be the Chief Volunteer Officer of The Corporation. The Board President shall lead the Board of Directors in performing its duties and responsibilities, including, if present, presiding at all meetings of the Board of Directors, and shall perform all other duties incident to the office or properly required by the Board of Directors.

6.05 Vice President

In the absence or disability of the Board President, the ranking Vice President or Vice President designated by the Board of Directors shall perform the duties of the Board President. When so acting, the Vice President shall have all the powers of and be subject to all the restrictions upon the Board President. The Vice President(s) shall have such other powers and perform such other duties prescribed for them by the Board of Directors or the Board President.

6.06 Secretary

The Secretary shall keep or cause to be kept a book of minutes of all meetings and actions of Directors and committees of Directors. The minutes of each meeting shall state the time and place that it was held and such other information as shall be necessary to determine the actions taken and whether the meeting was held in accordance with the law and these Bylaws. The Secretary shall cause notice to be given of all meetings of Directors as required by the Bylaws. The Secretary shall have such other powers and perform such other duties as may be prescribed by the Board of Directors or the Board President. The Secretary may appoint, with approval of the Board, a Director to assist in performance of all or part of the duties of the Secretary.

6.07 Treasurer

The Treasurer shall be the lead Director for oversight of the financial condition and affairs of The Corporation. The Treasurer shall oversee and keep the Board informed of the financial condition of The Corporation and of audit or financial review results. In conjunction with other Directors or officers, the Treasurer shall oversee budget preparation and shall ensure that appropriate financial reports, including an account of major transactions and the financial condition of The Corporation, are made available to the Board of Directors on a timely basis or as may be required by the Board of Directors. The Treasurer shall perform all duties properly required by the Board of Directors or the Board President. The Treasurer may appoint, with approval of the Board, a qualified fiscal agent or member of the staff to assist in performance of all or part of the duties of the Treasurer.

6.08 Non-Director Officers

The Board of Directors may designate additional officer positions of The Corporation and may appoint and assign duties to other non-Director officers of The Corporation.

ARTICLE VII
CONTRACTS, CHECKS, LOANS, INDEMNIFICATION AND RELATED MATTERS

7.01 Contracts and Other Writings

Except as otherwise provided by resolution of the Board or Board policy, all contracts, deeds, leases, mortgages, grants, and other agreements of The Corporation shall be executed on its behalf by the Treasurer or other persons to whom The Corporation has delegated authority to execute such documents in accordance with policies approved by the Board.

7.02 Checks, Drafts

All checks, drafts, or other orders for payment of money, notes, or other evidence of indebtedness issued in the name of The Corporation, shall be signed by such officer or officers, agent or agents, of The Corporation and in such manner as shall from time to time be determined by resolution of the Board.

7.03 Deposits

All funds of The Corporation not otherwise employed shall be deposited from time to time to the credit of The Corporation in such banks, trust companies, or other depository as the Board or a designated committee of the Board may select.

7.04 Loans

No loans shall be contracted on behalf of The Corporation, and no evidence of indebtedness shall be issued in its name unless authorized by resolution of the Board. Such authority may be general or confined to specific instances.

7.05 Indemnification

Mandatory Indemnification. The Corporation shall indemnify a Director or former Director, who was wholly successful, on the merits or otherwise, in the defense of any proceeding to which he or she was a party because he or she is or was a Director of The Corporation against reasonable expenses incurred by him or her in connection with the proceedings.

Permissible Indemnification. The Corporation shall indemnify a Director or former Director made a party to a proceeding because he or she is or was a Director of The Corporation, against liability incurred in the proceeding, if the determination to indemnify him or her has been made in the manner prescribed by the law and payment has been authorized in the manner prescribed by law.

Advance for Expenses. Expenses incurred in defending a civil or criminal action, suit or proceeding may be paid by The Corporation in advance of the final disposition of such action, suit or proceeding, as authorized by the Board of Directors in the specific case, upon receipt of (i) a written affirmation from the Director, officer, employee or agent of his or her good faith belief that he or she is entitled to indemnification as authorized in this Article, and (ii) an undertaking by or on behalf of the Director, officer, employee or agent to repay such amount, unless it shall ultimately be determined that he or she is entitled to be indemnified by The Corporation in these Bylaws.

Indemnification of Officers, Agents, and Employees. An officer of The Corporation who is not a Director is entitled to mandatory indemnification under this Article to the same extent as a Director. The Corporation may also indemnify and advance expenses to an employee or agent of The Corporation who is not a Director, consistent with the law of the state in which the nonprofit is incorporated and public policy, provided that such indemnification, and the scope of such indemnification, is set forth by the general or specific action of the Board or by contract.

ARTICLE VIII
MISCELLANEOUS

8.01 Books and Records

The Corporation shall keep correct and complete books and records of account and shall keep minutes of the proceedings of all meetings of its Board of Directors, a record of all actions taken by Board of Directors without a meeting, and a record of all actions taken by committees of the Board. In addition, The Corporation shall keep a copy of The Corporation's Articles of Incorporation and Bylaws as amended to date.

8.02 Fiscal Year

The fiscal year of The Corporation shall be from January 1 to December 31 of each year.

8.03 Conflict of Interest

The Board shall adopt and periodically review a Conflict of Interest Policy to protect The Corporation's interest when it is contemplating any transaction or arrangement which may benefit any Director, officer, employee, affiliate, or member of a committee with Board-delegated powers.

8.04 Bylaws Amendment

These Bylaws may be amended, altered, repealed, or restated by a vote of the majority of the Board of Directors then in office at a meeting of the Board, provided, however,

- a. that no amendment shall be made to these Bylaws which would cause The Corporation to cease to qualify as an exempt corporation under Section 501(c) (3) of the Internal Revenue Code, or the corresponding section of any future Federal tax code; and,
- b. that an amendment does not affect the voting rights of Directors. An amendment that does affect the voting rights of Directors further requires ratification by [choose between "a majority" or "a two-thirds"] vote of a quorum of Directors at a Board meeting.
- c. that all amendments be consistent with the Articles of Incorporation.

ARTICLE IX
COUNTERTERRORISM AND DUE DILIGENCE POLICY

In furtherance of its exemption by contributions to other organizations, domestic or foreign, The Corporation shall stipulate how the funds will be used and shall require the recipient to provide The Corporation with detailed records and financial proof of how the funds were utilized.

Although adherence and compliance with the U.S. Department of the Treasury's publication entitled the "Voluntary Best Practice for U.S.-Based Charities," is not mandatory, The Corporation willfully and voluntarily recognizes and puts into practice these guidelines and suggestions to reduce, develop, re-evaluate and strengthen a risk-based approach to guard against the threat of diversion of charitable funds or exploitation of charitable activity by terrorist organizations and their support networks.

The Corporation shall also comply and put into practice the federal guidelines, suggestions, laws and limitations set forth by pre-existing U.S. legal requirements related to combating terrorist financing, which include, but are not limited to, various sanctions programs administered by the Office of Foreign Assets Control (OFAC) in regard to its foreign activities.

ARTICLE X
DOCUMENT RETENTION POLICY

10.01 Purpose

The purpose of this Document Retention Policy is to establish standards for document integrity, retention, and destruction, and to promote the proper treatment of The Corporation's records.

10.02 Policy

Section 1. General Guidelines. Records should not be kept if they are no longer needed for the operation of the business or required by law. Unnecessary records should be eliminated from the files. The cost of maintaining records is an expense which can grow unreasonably if good housekeeping is not performed. A mass of records also makes it more difficult to find pertinent records. [Optional: "Where possible, the nonprofit shall adopt a digital, non-paper filing and retention system.]

From time to time, The Corporation may establish retention or destruction policies or schedules for specific categories of records in order to ensure legal compliance, and also to accomplish other objectives, such as preserving intellectual property and cost management. Several categories of documents that warrant special consideration are identified below. While minimum retention periods are established, the retention of the documents identified below and of documents not included in the identified categories should be determined primarily by the application of the general guidelines affecting document retention, as well as the exception for litigation relevant documents and any other pertinent factors.

Section 2. Exception for Litigation Relevant Documents. The Corporation expects all officers, Directors, and employees to comply fully with any published records retention or destruction policies and schedules, provided that all officers, Directors, and employees should note the following general exception to any stated destruction schedule: If you believe, or The Corporation informs you, that corporate records are relevant to litigation, or potential litigation (i.e., a dispute that could result in litigation), then you must preserve those records until it is determined that the records are no longer needed. That exception supersedes any previously or subsequently established destruction schedule for those records.

Section 3. Minimum Retention Periods for Specific Categories

   a. Corporate Documents. Corporate records include The Corporation's Articles of Incorporation, Bylaws, and IRS Application for Exemption. Corporate records should be retained permanently. IRS regulations require that the Form 1023 be available for public inspection upon request.
   b. Tax Records. Tax records include, but may not be limited to, documents concerning payroll, expenses, proof of contributions made by donors, accounting procedures, and other documents concerning The Corporation's revenues. Tax records should be retained for at least seven (7) years from the date of filing the applicable return.
   c. Employment Records/Personnel Records. State and federal statutes require The Corporation to keep certain recruitment,

employment, and personnel information. The Corporation should also keep personnel files that reflect performance reviews and any complaints brought against The Corporation or individual employees under applicable state and federal statutes. The Corporation should also keep in the employee's personnel file all final memoranda and correspondence reflecting performance reviews and actions taken by or against personnel. Employment applications should be retained for three (3) years. Retirement and pension records should be kept permanently. Other employment and personnel records should be retained for seven (7) years.

d. Board and Board Committee Materials. Meeting minutes should be retained in perpetuity in The Corporation's minute book. A clean copy of all other Board and Board Committee materials should be kept for no less than three (3) years by The Corporation.

e. Press Releases/Public Filings. The Corporation should retain permanent copies of all press releases and publicly filed documents under the theory that The Corporation should have its own copy to test the accuracy of any document a member of the public can theoretically produce against The Corporation.

f. Legal Files. Legal counsel should be consulted to determine the retention period of particular documents, but legal documents should generally be maintained for a period of ten (10) years.

g. Marketing and Sales Documents. The Corporation should keep final copies of marketing and sales documents for the same period of time it keeps other corporate files, generally three (3) years. An exception to the three-year policy may be sales invoices, contracts, leases, licenses, and other legal documentation. These documents should be kept for at least three (3) years beyond the life of the agreement.

h. Development/Intellectual Property and Trade Secrets. Development documents are often subject to intellectual

property protection in their final form (e.g., patents, trademarks, service marks, and copyrights). The documents detailing the development process are often also of value to The Corporation and are protected as trade secrets where The Corporation:
   i. derives independent economic value from the secrecy of the information; and
   ii. has taken affirmative steps to keep the information confidential.

The Corporation should keep all documents designated as containing trade secret information for at least the life of the trade secret.

i. Contracts. Final, execution copies of all contracts entered into by The Corporation should be retained. The Corporation should retain copies of the final contracts for at least three (3) years beyond the life of the agreement, and longer in the case of publicly filed contracts.
j. Correspondence. Unless correspondence falls under another category listed elsewhere in this policy, correspondence should generally be saved for two (2) years.
k. Banking and Accounting. Accounts payable ledgers and schedules should be kept for seven (7) years. Bank reconciliations, bank statements, deposit slips and checks (unless for important payments and purchases) should be kept for three (3) years. Any inventories of products, materials, and supplies and any invoices should be kept for seven (7) years.
l. Insurance. Expired insurance policies, insurance records, accident reports, claims, etc. should be kept permanently.
m. Audit Records. External audit reports should be kept permanently. Internal audit reports should be kept for three (3) years.

Section 4. Electronic Mail. E-mail that needs to be saved should be either:

i. printed in hard copy and kept in the appropriate file; or
ii. downloaded to a computer file and kept electronically or on removable drive as a separate file. The retention period depends upon the subject matter of the e-mail, as covered elsewhere in this policy.

ARTICLE XI
Transparency and Accountability
Disclosure of Financial Information With The General Public

11.01 Purpose

By making full and accurate information about its mission, activities, finances, and governance publicly available, The Corporation practices and encourages transparency and accountability to the general public. This Policy will:

a. indicate which documents and materials produced by The Corporation are presumptively open to staff and/or the public,
b. indicate which documents and materials produced by The Corporation are presumptively closed to staff and/or the public, and
c. specify the procedures whereby the open/closed status of documents and materials can be altered.

THE DETAILS OF THIS POLICY ARE AS FOLLOWS:

11.02 Financial and IRS documents (Form 1023 or 1023-EZ and the Form 990-series).

The Corporation shall provide its Internal Revenue Forms 990-series, 990-T, 1023 or 1023-EZ and 5227, Bylaws, Conflict of Interest Policy, and financial statements to the general public for inspection free of charge.

11.03 Means and Conditions of Disclosure

The Corporation shall have the option to make "Widely Available" the aforementioned documents on its internet website to be viewed and inspected by the general public when possible and practical to do so.

a. When made available electronically, the documents shall be posted in a format that allows an individual using the Internet to access, download, view and print them in a manner that exactly reproduces the image of the original document filed with the IRS (except information exempt from public disclosure requirements, such as contributor lists).
b. The website shall clearly inform readers that the document is available and provide instructions for downloading it.
c. The Corporation shall not charge a fee for downloading the information. Documents shall not be posted in a format that would require special computer hardware or software (other than software readily available to the public free of charge).
d. The Corporation shall inform anyone requesting the information where this information can be found, including the web address. This information must be provided immediately for in-person requests and within seven (7) days for mailed requests.

11.04 IRS Annual Information Returns (Form 990-series)

The Corporation shall submit the appropriate Form 990-series return to its Board of Directors prior to the filing of Form 990. While neither the approval of Form 990 or a review of the Form 990 is required under federal law, The Corporation's Form 990 shall be submitted to each member of the Board of Directors via hard copy or email at least ten (10) days before Form 990 is filed with the IRS.

11.05 Board

a. All Board deliberations shall be open to the public except where the Board passes a motion to make any specific portion confidential.
b. All Board minutes shall be open to the public once accepted by the Board, except where the Board passes a motion to make any specific portion confidential.
c. All papers and materials considered by the Board shall be open to the public following the meeting at which they are considered, except where the Board passes a motion to make any specific paper or material confidential.

11.06 Staff Records

a. All staff records shall be available for consultation by the staff member concerned or by their legal representatives.
b. No staff records shall be made available to any person outside The Corporation except the authorized governmental agencies.
c. Within The Corporation, staff records shall be made available only to those persons with managerial or personnel responsibilities for that staff member, except that staff records shall be made available to the Board when requested.

11.07 Donor Records

a. All donor records shall be available for consultation by the members and donors concerned or by their legal representatives.
b. No donor records shall be made available to any other person outside The Corporation except the authorized governmental agencies.
c. Within The Corporation, donor records shall be made available only to those persons with managerial or personnel responsibilities for dealing with those donors, except that donor records shall be made available to the Board when requested.

ARTICLE XII
CODE OF ETHICS AND WHISTLEBLOWER POLICY

12.01 Purpose

The Corporation requires and encourages Directors, officers and employees to observe and practice high standards of business and personal ethics in the conduct of their duties and responsibilities. The employees and representatives of The Corporation must practice honesty and integrity in fulfilling their responsibilities and comply with all applicable laws and regulations. It is the intent of The Corporation to adhere to all laws and regulations that apply to The Corporation, and the underlying purpose of this policy is to support The Corporation's goal of legal compliance. The support of all corporate staff is necessary to achieving compliance with various laws and regulations.

12.02 Reporting Violations

If any Director, officer, staff or employee reasonably believes that some policy, practice, or activity of The Corporation is in violation of law, a written complaint must be filed by that person with the Vice President or the Board President.

12.03 Acting in Good Faith

Anyone filing a complaint concerning a violation or suspected violation of a law or regulation must be acting in good faith and have reasonable grounds for believing the information disclosed indicates a violation. Any allegations that prove not to be substantiated and which prove to have been made maliciously or knowingly to be false shall be viewed as a serious disciplinary offense.

12.04 Retaliation

A person filing the aforesaid complaint is protected from retaliation only if she/he brings the alleged unlawful activity, policy, or practice to the attention of The Corporation and provides The Corporation with a reasonable opportunity to investigate and correct the alleged unlawful activity. The protection described below is only available to individuals that comply with this requirement.

The Corporation shall not retaliate against any Director, officer, staff or employee who in good faith, has made a protest or raised a complaint against some practice of The Corporation or of another individual or entity with whom The Corporation has a business relationship, on the basis of a reasonable belief that the practice is in violation of law or a clear mandate of public policy.

The Corporation shall not retaliate against any Director, officer, staff or employee who discloses or threatens to disclose to a supervisor or a public body, any activity, policy, or practice of The Corporation that the individual reasonably believes is in violation of a law or a rule, or regulation mandated pursuant to law or is in violation of a clear mandate of public policy concerning the health, safety, welfare, or protection of the environment.

12.05 Confidentiality

Violations or suspected violations may be submitted on a confidential basis by the complainant or may be submitted anonymously. Reports of violations or suspected violations shall be kept confidential to the extent possible, consistent with the need to conduct an adequate investigation.

12.06 Handling of Reported Violations

The Board President or Vice President shall notify the sender and acknowledge receipt of the reported violation or suspected violation within five business days. All reports shall be promptly investigated by the Board and its appointed committee, and appropriate corrective action shall be taken if warranted by the investigation.

This policy shall be made available to all Directors, officers, staffs or employees and they shall have the opportunity to ask questions about the policy.

ARTICLE XIII
AMENDMENT OF Articles of Incorporation

13.01 Amendment

Any amendment to the Articles of Incorporation may be adopted by approval of two-thirds (2/3) of the Board of Directors.

CERTIFICATE OF ADOPTION OF BYLAWS

I do hereby certify that the above stated Bylaws of The Corporation were approved by The Corporation's Board of Directors on_____ and constitute a complete copy of the Bylaws of The Corporation.

Secretary: _____

Date: _____

CHAPTER 12

DEVELOP A CONFLICT OF INTEREST POLICY

"Opportunities don't happen; you create them."
—Chris Grosser

SET PERSONAL INTERESTS ASIDE

IRS is concerned about conflicts of interest within 501(c) (3) corporations. A conflict of interest occurs when someone in a responsible position within a nonprofit has competing interests and is faced with making choices that could benefit themselves (or friends and family members) to the detriment of the organization. Board members and directors of a nonprofit have a first duty to promote the best interests of the organization. They must lay their personal interests aside when conducting the business of the nonprofit. Should a conflict of interest arise, it should be disclosed to the board of directors immediately.

> Board members and directors of a nonprofit have a first duty to promote the best interests of the organization.

Below is a template for the Conflict of Interest Policy from IRS containing the minimum requirements. In addition, IRS wants board members and directors to fill out an annual

Conflict of Interest Statement which should be kept on file with the corporation's other important documents. If you do not want to type out the template for the Conflict of Interest Policy or develop a Conflict of Interest Annual Statement, they are included in the Nonprofit Template Package Deal on our website at *www.doyourownnonprofit.com* *(*Proceeds go to *Pasture Valley Children Missions.)*

IRS SAMPLE CONFLICT OF INTEREST POLICY

CONFLICT OF INTEREST POLICY
[NAME OF ORGANIZATION]

Adopted on: _____

ARTICLE I
PURPOSE

The purpose of the conflict of interest policy is to protect [NAME OF ORGANIZATION] (the "Organization") interest when it is contemplating entering into a transaction or arrangement that might benefit the private interest of an officer or director of the Organization or might result in a possible excess benefit transaction. This policy is intended to supplement but not replace any applicable state and federal laws governing conflict of interest applicable to nonprofit and charitable organizations.

ARTICLE II
DEFINITIONS

1. Interested Person

Any director, principal officer, or member of a committee with governing board delegated powers, who has a direct or indirect financial interest, as defined below, is an interested person.

2. Financial Interest

A person has a financial interest if the person has, directly or indirectly, through business, investment, or family:

   a. An ownership or investment interest in any entity with which the Organization has a transaction or arrangement,
   b. A compensation arrangement with the Organization or with any entity or individual with which the Organization has a transaction or arrangement, or
   c. A potential ownership or investment interest in, or compensation arrangement with, any entity or individual with which the Organization is negotiating a transaction or arrangement.

Compensation includes direct and indirect remuneration as well as gifts or favors that are not insubstantial.

A financial interest is not necessarily a conflict of interest. Under Article III, Section 2, a person who has a financial interest may have a conflict of interest only if the appropriate governing board or committee decides that a conflict of interest exists.

ARTICLE III
PROCEDURES

1. Duty to Disclose

In connection with any actual or possible conflict of interest, an interested person must disclose the existence of the financial interest and be given the opportunity to disclose all material facts to the directors and members of committees with governing board delegated powers considering the proposed transaction or arrangement.

2. Determining Whether a Conflict of Interest Exists

After disclosure of the financial interest and all material facts, and after any discussion with the interested person, s/he shall leave the governing board or committee meeting while the determination of a conflict of interest is discussed and voted upon. The remaining board or committee members shall decide if a conflict of interest exists.

3. Procedures for Addressing the Conflict of Interest

a. An interested person may make a presentation at the governing board or committee meeting, but after the presentation, s/he shall leave the meeting during the discussion of, and the vote on, the transaction or arrangement involving the possible conflict of interest.
b. The chairperson of the governing board or committee shall, if appropriate, appoint a disinterested person or committee to investigate alternatives to the proposed transaction or arrangement.

c. After exercising due diligence, the governing board or committee shall determine whether the Organization can obtain with reasonable efforts a more advantageous transaction or arrangement from a person or entity that would not give rise to a conflict of interest.
d. If a more advantageous transaction or arrangement is not reasonably possible under circumstances not producing a conflict of interest, the governing board or committee shall determine by a majority vote of the disinterested directors whether the transaction or arrangement is in the Organization's best interest, for its own benefit, and whether it is fair and reasonable. In conformity with the above determination, it shall make its decision as to whether to enter into the transaction or arrangement.

4. Violations of the Conflicts of Interest Policy

a. If the governing board or committee has reasonable cause to believe a member has failed to disclose actual or possible conflicts of interest, it shall inform the member of the basis for such belief and afford the member an opportunity to explain the alleged failure to disclose.
b. If, after hearing the member's response and after making further investigation as warranted by the circumstances, the governing board or committee determines the member has failed to disclose an actual or possible conflict of interest, it shall take appropriate disciplinary and corrective action.

ARTICLE IV
RECORDS OF PROCEEDINGS

The minutes of the governing board and all committees with board delegated powers shall contain:

a. The names of the persons who disclosed or otherwise were found to have a financial interest in connection with an actual or possible conflict of interest, the nature of the financial interest, any action taken to determine whether a conflict of interest was present, and the governing board or committee's decision as to whether a conflict of interest in fact existed.
b. The names of the persons who were present for discussions and votes relating to the transaction or arrangement, the content of the discussion, including any alternatives to the proposed transaction or arrangement, and a record of any votes taken in connection with the proceedings.

ARTICLE V
COMPENSATION

a. A voting member of the governing board who receives compensation, directly or indirectly, from the Organization for services is precluded from voting on matters pertaining to that member's compensation.
b. A voting member of any committee whose jurisdiction includes compensation matters and who receives compensation, directly or indirectly, from the Organization for services is precluded from voting on matters pertaining to that member's compensation.
c. No voting member of the governing board or any committee whose jurisdiction includes compensation matters and who receives compensation, directly or indirectly, from the Organization, either individually or collectively, is prohibited from providing information to any committee regarding compensation.

ARTICLE VI
ANNUAL STATEMENTS

Each director, principal officer and member of a committee with governing board delegated powers shall annually sign a statement which affirms such person:

a. Has received a copy of the conflict of interest policy,
b. Has read and understands the policy,
c. Has agreed to comply with the policy, and
d. Understands the Organization is charitable and in order to maintain its federal tax exemption, it must engage primarily in activities which accomplish one or more of its tax-exempt purposes.

ARTICLE VII
REVIEWS

To ensure the Organization operates in a manner consistent with charitable purposes and does not engage in activities that could jeopardize its tax-exempt status, periodic reviews shall be conducted. The periodic reviews shall, at a minimum, include the following subjects:

a. Whether compensation arrangements and benefits are reasonable, based on competent survey information, and the result of arm's length bargaining,
b. Whether partnerships, joint ventures, and arrangements with management organizations conform to the Organization's written policies, are properly recorded, reflect reasonable investment or payments for goods and services, further charitable purposes and do not result in inurement, impermissible private benefit or in an excess benefit transaction.

ARTICLE VIII
USE OF OUTSIDE EXPERTS

When conducting the periodic reviews as provided for in Article VII, the Organization may, but need not, use outside advisors. If outside experts are used, their use shall not relieve the governing board of its responsibility for ensuring periodic reviews are conducted.

In addition to the Conflict of Interest Policy, you need to create a Conflict of Interest Annual Statement for board members (and managers and employees if desired) to sign. One might look something like this 2-page document:

PERSONAL AND CONFIDENTIAL
[NAME OF ORGANIZATION]

Conflict of Interest Statement

1. As a(n) _____ of this Organization, I acknowledge that I:

    a. Received a copy of the Organization's Conflict of Interest Policy dated _____ _____, 20_____.
    b. Read and understood the policy;
    c. Agree to comply with the spirit and intent of the policy and will disclose any potential conflicts, other than those stated on next page, as they may arise before completion of my next conflict of interest statement; and

d. Understand that the Organization is a charitable organization, and in order to maintain its federal tax exemption, it must engage primarily in activities which accomplish one or more of its tax-exempt purposes.

2. Based on a review of the Organization's Conflict of Interest Policy, are you aware of any interest that you or a related person may have that could give rise to a conflict of interest? If yes, please complete Attachment A to this form.

    _____Yes   _____No

My answers above are accurately stated to the best of my knowledge and belief.

Dated   _____
Signature   _____
Printed Name   _____

PERSONAL AND CONFIDENTIAL
[NAME OF ORGANIZATION]

Conflict of Interest Statement

Attachment A

1. Please list all relationships (if any) between you or a "related party" (as defined below) with the Organization that involve an actual or potential financial benefit to you or the related party or that otherwise may represent a conflict of interest within the spirit and intent of the policy. Include an estimate of the related actual or potential financial benefit.

_____
_____
_____
_____
_____
_____
_____

2. Please list any business dealings during the past year (or, as applicable, since your last submission of this Conflict of Interest Statement) of which you are aware in which you or a "related party" (as defined below) have received a salary, gifts, or loans from any source from which the Organization obtains goods or services or otherwise has business dealings:

_____
_____
_____
_____
_____

3. Please list any potential or pending transaction to which the Organization is a party and in which you or a "related party" (as defined below) has a direct or indirect interest.

_____

_____

_____

_____

_____

_____

_____

NOTE: A "related party" (as defined in this policy) is a family member; a business or organization of which the person signing this statement or a family member owns or expects to own, directly or indirectly, more than a 5% interest; has a beneficial interest in a trust that owns directly or indirectly more than a 5% interest; or is a director, officer, or employee. A "family member" is a parent (or more remote ancestor), spouse, brother, sister, spouse of a brother or sister, child, step-child, grandchild, great-grandchild or spouse of a child, step-child, grandchild or great-grandchild of the person signing this statement.

CHAPTER 13

HOLD AND DOCUMENT THE FIRST BOARD MEETING

"You miss 100% of the shots you don't take."
—Wayne Gretzky

Did you know that IRS and auditors consider board meeting minutes as legal documents that will hold up in court? Many legal minds believe that if it is not in the meeting minutes, it did not occur because the meeting minutes are formal records of the business conducted and the decisions made by an organization.

There is no set format for meeting minutes, and each organization should decide how the meeting minutes should look. When secretaries of the board change, the format often changes to suit the new secretary. As long as the required information is recorded, the format is not critical. Copies of meeting minutes from previous meetings should be given to board members for review and approval. All meeting minutes should be filed in a safe, accessible place.

> **As long as the required information is recorded, the format is not critical.**

There are some things that should be included in every set of meeting minutes:

1. Name of the organization
2. Date and time of the meeting
3. Who ran the meeting
4. Who was there and who was absent
5. What was voted on and whether anyone abstained from voting
6. All motions made
7. When the meeting ended
8. Who prepared the meeting minutes

Personal opinions and heated arguments or discussions should not be included. Minutes should cover the business of the organization, not document disagreements among members. Do not include in-depth details of reports, better to just attach the reports to the minutes.

If you are about to conduct your first board meeting, you want to include the business of setting up the organization and getting it running. Your meeting minutes should include the following:

1. Initial board members and the offices, if any, that they hold (for example president, vice president, secretary, treasurer, or board member)
2. How you will elect or appoint board members in the future (successors can be appointed by the existing board members)
3. Approve application for an FEIN number (if not already done)
4. Approve development and submission of Articles of Incorporation (if not already done)
5. Adopt the organization's bylaws
6. Approve applying for 501(c)(3) status with IRS

7. Approve setting up banking accounts and decide how funds will be handled, and who is authorized to conduct banking activities and who can sign checks
8. Approve the Conflict of Interest Policy
9. Determine fiscal accounting year

Your board meeting minutes and any resolutions about banking that were approved at board meetings may be needed to open a bank account. Many banks need proof of who can sign checks and conduct the banking business for the organization. Your board meeting minutes show who is in which office and can list who is allowed to do banking business. As a courtesy, I included an Initial Organizational Meeting Minutes template as part of the package deal under the state templates tab at *www.doyourownnonprofit.org* if you don't want to create your own from scratch. All proceeds go to Pasture Valley Children Missions.

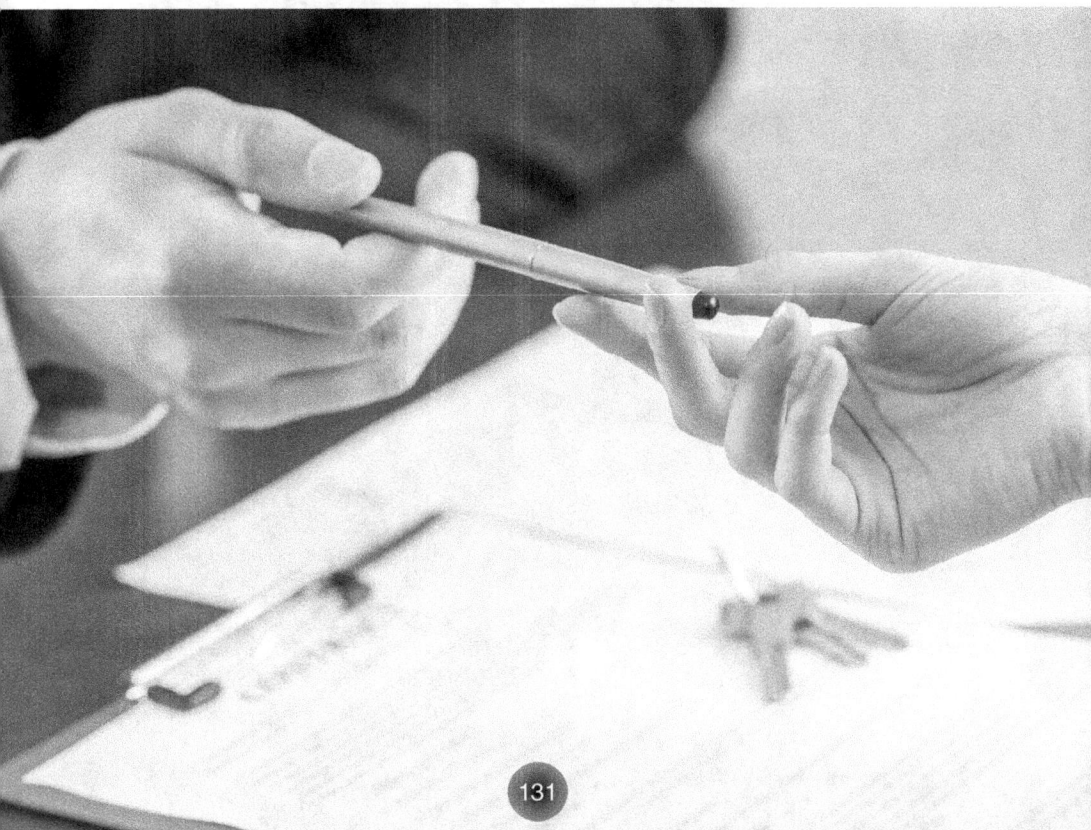

PART II

NEW ONLINE ONLY IRS FORM 1023 APPLICATION FOR TAX-EXEMPT STATUS

CHAPTER 14

REQUEST FOR RECOGNITION OF EXEMPTION

"Whether you think you can or think you can't, you're right."

—Henry Ford

WHERE TO BEGIN

If you have completed all the requirements in previous chapters, you are ready to complete the federal application. IRS applications **must** *be filed online only* effective January 31, 2020, and you have two choices of which form to use based on mission, where you operate in the world, and projected budget. Both applications are available at ***www.pay.gov***

Your choices are:

> **IRS Form 1023**, *Application for Recognition of Exemption under Section 501(c) (3) of the Internal Revenue Code* for organizations with projected annual revenues over $50K within the next three years, schools, churches, hospitals, research facilities, or if the organization will be working, partnering, or has/will have board members outside the United States. (Start with the next chapter.)

IRS Form 1023-EZ, *Streamlined Application for Recognition of Exemption Under Section 501(c) (3) of the Internal Revenue Code* for organizations with projected annual budgets under $50K for the next three years, with no international activities, partners or board members, and the organization is not a church, school, hospital, or research facility. (Skip to Chapter 32.)

The IRS forms in use at the time of publication and for which this book covers are:

- Form 1023: January 2020
- Form 1023-EZ: October 2018

It is possible that IRS will update the forms again. If you get a later version, use this book for the general categories of answers, but put the answers in the correct section of any new form.

Information on the Form 1023-EZ is in Part IV of this book. The rest of Part II and all of Part III deals with Form 1023, *Application for Recognition of Exemption under Section 501(c) (3) of the Internal Revenue Code* and required schedules.

WHAT TO EXPECT

Once you submit your application package to IRS electronically, you will get a letter about 45 days later acknowledging receipt of the application, and letting you know that IRS will process it one of two ways: fast or slow. They do not tell you which one! You get a form letter that everyone gets, and there is no reason to stress over whether they will assign an agent. Even if they do, it is only to ask some additional questions.

Wait about three months after that initial letter for IRS to send you a *determination letter*. It is called a determination letter because the first sentence says, "We are pleased to tell you that we have *determined* you're exempt from federal income tax under Internal Revenue Code (IRC) Section 501(c) (3)." The wording changes from time to time, but the meaning is the same. The determination letter is a form letter that looks very much like the FEIN confirmation letter.

IRS says it can take 6 – 12 months to process your application, but if you use the instructions in this book, you should hear back in 3 – 4 months. As long as you file within 27 months of getting incorporated by the state, your 501(c) (3) status will be effective the date the state approved your nonprofit status. IRS backdates it so that there is no gap in 501(c) (3) coverage. If you file after 27 months from the date of incorporation with the state, IRS does not backdate the application and approves 501(c) (3) tax-exempt status with a current effective date.

If you happen to misplace your determination letter, IRS is now posting (past and present) determination letters and tax returns online (at least some of the time; they have been remiss in updating some documents after the government shutdown in 2019). You can access a copy of your determination letter by doing an internet search for *Tax Exempt Organization Search* or by going to *https://apps.irs.gov/app/eos/*.

If the determination letter is not posted for whatever reason and you have lost your copy, you send IRS Form 4506-A to get another copy. It takes up to 60 days. The determination letter is your proof that you have 501(c) (3) tax-exempt status and is required for grants and is a public record that anyone can have a copy of or ask to see. You are obligated by IRS regulations to give anyone who asks copies of your federal filing, your annual returns, and your determination letter from IRS. It is a condition of getting tax-exempt 501(c) (3) status. Luckily, IRS posts the determination letter and tax returns online, so you can direct anyone who asks to the IRS website.

IMPORTANT!

If you do not hear from IRS within about 60 - 90 days from the time they send the letter acknowledging they got your package, call them at 877-829-5500. You will need your FEIN when you call. We have had dozens of cases in which IRS agents said they sent follow-up questionnaires or determination letters that never arrived. In the case of a questionnaire, IRS gives you a deadline to answer. If you don't get the notice, you don't answer it. In that case, IRS takes your money, cancels your application and says, "Oh well..." Check on it if you don't hear back in 60 days or so after the form letter that says they got your package. It is a precaution to avoid IRS bureaucracy and unnecessary additional costs. Best to call early in the day. By afternoon, you normally get a recording that says, "due to high call volumes, your call will not go through; please call another day."

If your application contains everything IRS needs to know, a determination letter will be issued. If not, you will receive a request for additional clarification or information. Needing more information can delay approval, but not the effective date. If you apply within 27 months from the time you incorporated in the state, it will be the day the state approved your incorporation no matter when IRS gets around to approving your application.

> **If your application contains everything IRS needs to know, a determination letter will be issued.**

You can get expedited handling if you request it for a compelling reason. To ask for expedited handling, you will write and attach a letter to the online application requesting priority approval and give a good, compelling reason for asking. Good, compelling reasons include:

- pending grants of a substantial amount ($5,000 or more is normally adequate) that will not be made without 501(c)

(3) status and for which there is a deadline at which time the funds will be lost;
- your organization is created to provide relief to victims of disasters such as recent floods, hurricanes, tsunamis, tornadoes, or situations such as the Coronavirus; or
- your application has been delayed because of problems at IRS due to no fault of your organization.

IRS estimates that it takes over 100 hours to complete the 501(c) (3) process. Hopefully, this book will cut down those hours by more than half, but grit your teeth, get ready to dig in, and describe your organization completely so that a quick determination can be made without required follow-up from IRS. If you put in the work up front to do it right the first time, you will not have to deal with ongoing correspondence and paperwork from IRS.

DISCLOSURE

Did you know that you are allowed to see and have copies of Form 1023 for most nonprofit organizations that have been approved after July 15, 1987? You can be charged a fair price for making copies. Not all organizations know they are required to disclose their applications, so you can ask for a copy of the paperwork and quote the IRS guidance located at *www.irs.gov* (search for Public Disclosure and Availability of Exempt Organizations Returns and Applications: Documents Subject to Public Disclosure) which states (last updated on January 8, 2020):

Public Disclosure and Availability of Exempt Organizations Returns and Applications: Documents Subject to Public Disclosure

What tax documents must an exempt organization make available for public inspection and copying?

An exempt organization must make available for public inspection its exemption application. An exemption application includes the Form 1023 (PDF) or Form 1023-EZ (for organizations recognized as exempt under Internal Revenue Code section 501(c) (3)), Form 1024 (PDF) or Form 1024-A (PDF), as applicable, (for organizations recognized as exempt under most other paragraphs of section 501(c)), or the letter submitted under the paragraphs for which no form is prescribed, together with supporting documents and any letter or document issued by the IRS concerning the application. A political organization exempt from taxation under section 527(a) must make available for public inspection and copying its notice of status, Form 8871.

In addition, an exempt organization must make available for public inspection and copying its annual return. Such returns include Form 990, Return of Organization Exempt From Income Tax (PDF), Form 990-EZ, Short Form Return of Organization Exempt From Income Tax (PDF), Form 990-PF, Return of Private Foundation (PDF), Form 990-BL, Information and Initial Excise Tax Return for Black Lung Benefit Trusts and Certain Related Persons (PDF), and the Form 1065, U.S. Partnership Return of Income (PDF).

A section 501(c) (3) organization must make available for public inspection and copying any Form 990-T, Exempt Organization Business Income Tax Return (PDF), filed after August 17, 2006. Returns must be available for a three-year period beginning with the due date of the return (including any extension of time for filing). For this purpose, the **return** *includes any schedules, attachments, or supporting documents that relate to the imposition of tax on the unrelated business* income of the charity. See *Public Inspection and Disclosure of Form 990-T* for more information.

A section 501(c)(4) organization is not required to disclose Form 8976 – Notice of Intent to Operate Under Section 501(c)(4). See Revenue Procedure 2016-41 for more information.

An exempt organization is not required to disclose Schedule K-1 of Form 1065 (PDF) or Schedule A of *Form 990-BL (PDF)*. With the exception of private foundations, an exempt organization is not required to disclose the name and address of any contributor to the organization.

Many organizations choose to meet the disclosure requirements by putting their public documents online. However, with the new online filing system effective January 31, 2020, IRS may start posting the applications online. The reasoning for the new online only applications included faster processing and more transparency to the public.

If you contact an organization and they do not give you a copy of their paperwork, you can make a stink and report them. But why bother? Instead, use a Form 4506-A and ask IRS for a copy. They take up to 60 days to send it, but you can get a copy. It is free up to 100 pages, and twenty cents a page over 100 pages. Fill out the form, check Form 1023 in Box 9 and either mail or fax it to:

Internal Revenue Service
Attn: Correspondence Unit
P.O. Box 2508, Room 4024
Cincinnati, OH 45201
Fax Number (855) 204-6184

CHAPTER 15

PART I

IDENTIFICATION OF APPLICANT

*"Setting a goal is not the main thing.
It is deciding how you will go about achieving it
and staying with that plan."*

—Tom Landry

ONE STEP AT A TIME

You are now ready to begin filling out the actual application. No need to be overwhelmed – simply take it one step at a time, and you will get through this. If you are unsure of what to put in any section of the Form 1023, call IRS Tax Exempt and Government Entities Customer Account Services at (877) 829-5500. Better to ask now than to delay the approval of your application for months.

> **IMPORTANT NOTE:** You cannot use many forms of punctuation in the online application. For example, you cannot use contractions at all. If you type in *children's*, your entry will be rejected. You must type in *childrens* instead.

Start by going to *www.pay.gov* and setting up an account. It is fast and easy. Remember your login information because you can work on your application, save it, and go back to it later. For narrative answers, you might want to write or type out your answers first, then copy and paste them into the boxes provided. Use *Control* + *V* simultaneously to paste into the application narrative boxes. (On Apple computers, use *Command* Key + *P* keys).

We strongly suggest that you:

- Print a copy or save a copy of the application to your computer in case the online copy gets lost, you cannot get logged in to the IRS site to continue the application, or anything else that might cause you to have to start over. Better to be safe than have to do it over.
- Once you complete the application, you will need to submit copies of your Articles of Incorporation (by whatever name your state calls the incorporation), your ADOPTED bylaws (meaning you need to have a date of approval on them), and anything that will not fit in the narrative boxes in the application. If you start to fill out a section and just do not have enough room to say all you need to say, write "See Attached", then type the question numbers and the answers in a Word or similar document. You will need to combine all the documents into one PDF (Articles, bylaws, and answers) into one document to upload with your application. Some Adobe PDF programs have the "Organize" function to combine documents. If not, scan all the documents at once into one document to attach to the application. If you do not have the software or equipment to do that, ask a computer-savvy friend to combine the documents. You might also call your local office supply store such as Staples and ask them to help you.

Below we have listed what is needed for each specific line in the application:

Line 1a. Full name of organization (exactly as it appears in your organizing document and FEIN)

Enter your organization's name from state incorporation document, including any name change amendments. Be sure to include Inc. or Corp. if that is part of the organization's official name. Do not abbreviate or use acronyms – spell out the complete name as it is listed on the approved state incorporation or name change amendment.

Line 1b. c/o Name (if applicable)

If you want a specific person to be the go-to person for correspondence, put in an *in-care-of* name here. If you are the founder and are using your personal address, it makes sense to use your name. You can also leave it blank.

Line 1c. Mailing Address (Number, street and room/suite)

This will be the address you want correspondence sent to. A post office box is fine if that is where you get your mail.

Line 1d. City

List the city that goes with the address in Line 1c.

Line 1e. Country

Use the dropdown menu for United States (or other country if applicable).

Line 1f. State

Use the dropdown menu for your state.

Line 1g. Zip Code + 4

If you do not know the +4, just enter the zip code.

Line 1h. Foreign Province or State

Enter the province or state (spell out, no abbreviations) where you want mail sent (if applicable). If not, leave blank.

Line 1i. Foreign Postal Code

Enter the foreign postal code for the province or state where you want mail sent to (if applicable). If not, leave blank.

Line 2. Employer Identification Number

Enter the EIN (also called FEIN) issued by IRS. It is 9-digits long: the first 2 digits, a dash, and the last 7 digits. For example, the EIN for Pasture Valley Children Missions (a nonprofit Kitty founded) is 35-2468924. If you do not have an FEIN number, go back to Chapter 6 and follow the instructions. You can get a number online from IRS. IRS does not accept applications for organizations without FEIN numbers. If you cannot get the FEIN online, you can mail or fax IRS Form SS-4 and IRS will issue a number and either fax or mail it back to you.

Line 3. Month Tax Year Ends

Your accounting year should end at a logical point. For example, a school organization may end on June 30 or July 31. Most other organizations have December 31 as the accounting period end. Use the dropdown menu to select the month in which you plan to end your annual accounting period. The last day of the accounting period will be the last day of the month you select. Also, check your bylaws to verify the accounting period. Depending on the month you select, your first accounting period may be less than one calendar year. For example, if you start your nonprofit in May and your accounting year ends in December, you will only have a seven-month accounting period the first year. This is not a problem. DO NOT select your accounting period based on the month you incorporate. That has nothing to do with the accounting period. The first year is normally less than 12 months.

Line 4. Person to Contact if More Information is Needed (officer, director, trustee, or authorized representative)

Who do you want IRS to talk with if they need to discuss your application, organizational documents, bylaws, or other such matters? This person can be an officer, director, or any other person you designate to discuss your organization's rules and procedures. It can also be you. Another option is to designate an authorized representative, attorney, or accountant to represent you by uploading an IRS Form 2848 with your other application documents.

Line 5. Contact Phone Number

What is the contact person's phone number? Include the area code.

Line 6. Fax Number (optional)

Enter fax number if you have one.

Line 7. User Fee Submitted

The user fee will be $600 and can be paid by credit card or bank withdrawal.

Line 8. Organization's Website (if available):

If you have a website that is complete and operational and the content matches the mission you are giving IRS, list it. If you are still working on it or don't have one, leave it blank. If you have a website, IRS will often send a written request for you to make copies of the webpages and forward them to the IRS agent working on your application. If you don't have a website or if it is not active yet, there is nothing to send for and thus no delay in processing.

Line 9. List the names, titles, and mailing addresses of your officers, directors, and/or trustees.

Give board information on each officer, director, etc. You can use the organization mailing address for the board members. If you have more than five board members, check the box for additional members. A narrative box will open, and you type in the names, titles and addresses of the additional board members.

This completes Part I of the application. Ready to go on to Part II?

CHAPTER 16

PART II

ORGANIZATIONAL STRUCTURE

"Success is no accident. It is hard work, perseverance, learning, studying, sacrifice and most of all, love of what you are doing or learning to do."

—Pele

This section of the application has to do with your organizational structure. Your organization must be a corporation, one specific type of Limited Liability Corporation (LLC), or a trust in order to be eligible for 501(c)(3) status. In this section, you must select your form of organization. You will also be required to attach your organizational documents before submitting the application online.

> In this section, you must select your form of organization.

Line 1. You must be a corporation, limited liability company (LLC), unincorporated association, or trust to be tax exempt.

Select your type of organization.

Choice 1: Corporation
If you are following the guidance in this book, select Corporation.

IRS defines a corporation as:

> "an entity organized under a Federal or state statute, or a statute of a federally recognized Indian tribal or Alaskan native government."

Corporation is the most popular and frequent organizational structure for 501(c)(3) status. You get corporate status by filing Articles of Incorporation (by whatever name a state calls it: Charter, Certificate of Formation, Articles of Organization, Certificate of Incorporation, or Articles of Incorporation) with the state (see Chapters 9 and 10). The state approves your paperwork and assigns the date you became a corporate entity. You must include an exact copy of your approved document with the Form 1023, as well as any amendments to the original document. If you do not have an exact copy, you can contact the state corporation division for another copy.

Choice 2: Limited Liability Corporation
Not all Limited Liability Corporations or Companies are eligible for 501(c)(3) status. To qualify, all the members of an LLC must be other 501(c)(3) organizations. LLCs made up of individuals are not eligible for tax-exempt status. LLCs are owned by members; nonprofit organizations are not owned; they are separate entities. This structure of LLC organization is confusing, contradictory, and brings problems you may not want to try to solve. If you are contemplating LLC structure, contact an attorney for further guidance to avoid laborious paperwork with IRS and extended timeframe for approval (or outright rejection of your application).

Choice 3: Unincorporated Association
An unincorporated association must have a written agreement laying out the purpose of the association. There must be at least two members. According to IRS instructions, *"the articles*

of organization of an unincorporated association must include the name of your organization, your purpose, the date the document was adopted, and the signatures of at least two individuals." Date of adoption is important to IRS.

Choice 4: Trust
A trust can be established by a will or by a trust agreement or declaration of trust. If created by a will, a copy of the death certificate and a copy of pertinent parts of the will must be attached to the application. A trust involves three groups of people:

- The donor(s)
- The trustee(s)
- The beneficiaries

Trustees can be sued on behalf of the trust. Not all trust instruments and structures are eligible for 501(c)(3) status.

Line 2. Enter the date you formed. (MM/DD/YYYY)

This is the date that the state approved your incorporation. It may not be the same day you signed the incorporation document. Look on the articles of incorporation for the effective date. When in doubt, call the corporations division and ask.

Line 3. Select your state (or U.S. territory) of incorporation or other formation. If you were formed under the laws of a foreign country, select Foreign Country.

Use the dropdown to select your state. Do not select a foreign country because you plan to work in that country. You select the state you incorporated in.

Line 4. Have you adopted bylaws? If "Yes," at the end of this form, upload a current copy showing the date of adoption. If "No," explain how you select your officers, directors, or trustees.

If you have bylaws, mark "Yes" and attach them at the end of your application before submitting. IRS does not require them, but if you do not have them, some of their questions about how you function as an organization will not be answered. In that case, they may not approve your application without further information. This could delay your application. Be safe, send the bylaws and eliminate the delay.

Your other choice to is explain how you select your officers, directors, or trustees in the narrative box provided. You can say that existing board directors select replacement board directors, and that the board votes (or membership if you have a membership group – most nonprofits do not have memberships) on the officers every year (or two years if you prefer).

Line 5. Are you a successor to another organization? Answer "Yes" if you have taken or will take over the activities of another organization, you took over 25% or more of the fair market value of the net assets of another organization, or you were established upon the conversion of an organization from for-profit to nonprofit status. If "Yes," complete Schedule G.

If you are setting up from scratch, mark "No." If you are taking over another organization, mark "Yes" and see Chapter 30 for guidance on Schedule G.

CHAPTER 17

PART III

REQUIRED PROVISIONS IN YOUR ORGANIZING DOCUMENT

"The difference between a successful person and others is not a lack of strength, not a lack of knowledge, but rather a lack of will."

—Vince Lombardi

Line 1. Section 501(c)(3) requires that your organizing document limit your purposes to one or more exempt purposes within section 501(c)(3), such as charitable, religious, educational, and/or scientific purposes.

The following is an example of an acceptable purpose clause: The organization is organized exclusively for charitable, religious, educational, and scientific purposes under section 501(c)(3) of the Internal Revenue Code, or corresponding section of any future federal tax code.

Does your organizing document meet this requirement?

If you filed your incorporation using guidelines in Chapter 10, your document contains the required purpose clause. Answer "Yes." If you did not include the purpose clause, you will need to file an amendment to the state incorporation before applying to IRS for 501(c) (3) tax-exempt status.

Line 1a. State specifically where your organizing document meets this requirement, such as a reference to a particular article or section in your organizing document (Page/Article/Paragraph):

Your organizing document must contain a purpose clause that is consistent with IRS requirements. This question wants to know exactly where it is located in your incorporation document. Here is what you are looking for in your state Articles of Incorporation (different states call it different names such as Charter, Certificate of Formation, Certificate of Incorporation, or Articles of Association):

> *Said Corporation is organized exclusively for charitable, religious, educational, and scientific purposes, including, for such purposes, the making of distributions to organizations that qualify as exempt organizations under Section 501(c) (3) of the Internal Revenue Code, or the corresponding section of any future federal tax code.*

Find that statement in your Articles and put the page, article, and paragraph in the box.

Line 2. The following is an example of an acceptable dissolution clause: Upon the dissolution of this organization, assets shall be distributed for one or more exempt purposes within the meaning of section 501(c) (3) of the Internal Revenue Code, or corresponding section of any future federal tax code, or shall

be distributed to the federal government, or to a state or local government, for a public purpose.

Section 501(c) (3) requires that your organizing document provide that upon dissolution, your remaining assets be used exclusively for section 501(c) (3) exempt purposes, such as charitable, religious, educational, and/or scientific purposes. Depending on your entity type and the state in which you are formed, this requirement may be satisfied by operation of state law. Does your organizing document meet this requirement?

To be approved for nonprofit status by IRS, you must have a dissolution clause that states that if you stop being a tax-exempt organization, all your assets will be given to another nonprofit organization. Here is what you are looking for as a dissolution clause (some IRS agents have accepted the first sentence only, but many agents look for the whole thing):

> *Upon the dissolution of the corporation, assets shall be distributed for one or more exempt purposes within the meaning of Section 501(c) (3) of the Internal Revenue Code, or corresponding section of any future federal tax code, or shall be distributed to the federal government, or to a state or local government, for a public purpose. Any such assets not so disposed of shall be disposed of by a Court of Competent Jurisdiction of the county in which the principal office of the corporation is then located, exclusively for such purposes or to such organization or organizations as said Court shall determine which are organized and operated exclusively for such purposes.*

If you used this book to complete your state incorporation, you can mark "Yes" to this question. If you didn't use this book and filed without a dissolution clause, you may need to file an amendment if you are not in a state that relies on operation of state law for dissolution. You can find information on those states at *https://www.irs.gov/charities-non-profits/charitable-organizations/required-provisions-for-organizing-documents-operation-by-state-law*

Line 2a. Location of Dissolution Clause. State specifically where your organizing document meets this requirement, such as a reference to a particular article or section in your organizing document (Page/Article/Paragraph) or indicate that you rely on state law.

From your organizing document, list the page, article, and paragraph of the dissolution clause. If you relied on operation of state law (not applicable if you used this book for guidance), type "Operation of State Law" in the box.

CHAPTER 18

PART IV

YOUR ACTIVITIES

*"If you can't explain it simply,
you don't understand it well enough."*
—Albert Einstein

THE HEART OF THE APPLICATION

You have come to the heart of your application, and it is now time to touch the heart of the IRS agent who will process your package. This is your chance to describe the mission you are undertaking to do good things in the world. The key to getting your application approved lies in your willingness to put forth the effort to make your vision come alive. You must answer the questions in the IRS agent's mind; not just the ones on the application, but the other ones that any interested person would want to know when finding out about your mission.

What do you tell people about your organization when you are explaining it one-on-one or in a small group? How did your organization come into existence? What was the deciding impetus that led to its creation? What excites you most about it? Who is involved? What are their qualifications? What do you want to accomplish? How are you going to accomplish it? How will you pay for it (make sure this information agrees with your financial section of the application)? How will you select the people, groups, or organizations you will help?

Remember to answer the questions asked on the application in enough detail to answer the *Who, What, When, Where, How, How Much,* and *Why* of each question.

NO RIGHT OR WRONG WAY

There is no right or wrong way to format this section, but use positive, powerful terms and word choices. Don't limit your future growth, but at the same time, do not take on the world. For example, do not say you are going to provide laptop computers to three rural schools in Alabama. Later you may want to provide iPads or work with schools in Mississippi as well. Instead, you might say you are going to improve technology access to rural schools in the southern United States, beginning with providing laptop computers to three rural schools in Alabama. In this activities section, your narrative can show a small start, and give your organization room to grow so that you don't have to go back later and ask IRS to approve expanding your mission. Make it big now and grow into it later.

TELL YOUR STORY

Tell a story with your words and weave in the important points as part of the story. Be careful in this section not to refer to the organization with ownership; it is a separate entity that is not owned by anyone. Another way to get your mission across is to add copies of brochures, flyers, handouts, printed copies of website pages, and any other written material that will expand the IRS agent's understanding of what you are trying to do. If you choose to add these things, they will be part of the upload of required documents at the end of the application. You get to upload one document only, so all the items you want to add must be send in one combined document. You may also want to add short biographies of the board of directors demonstrating how they are qualified to perform the organization's mission or attach a resume or curriculum vitae for each board member to the application package. Why? Because sometimes IRS comes back and asks for a resume showing at least three years employment and address information. Best to put it in the first time and avoid any potential delay in processing.

Line 1. Describe completely and in detail your past, present, and planned activities. Do not refer to or repeat the purposes in your organizing document. For each past, present, or planned activity, include information that answers the following questions:

- a. **What is the activity?**
- b. **Who conducts the activity?**
- c. **Where is the activity conducted?**
- d. **What percentage of your total time is allocated to the activity?**
- e. **How is the activity funded (for example, donations, fees, etc.) and what percentage of your overall expenses is allocated to this activity?**
- f. **How does the activity further your exempt purposes?**

One way to answer this question is to organize your activities in a list of most time and funding to least time and funding and assign a percentage of time and a percentage of expenses to each activity. It is a guess, so don't worry if the percentages are off in real life. Another way to answer is to write a narrative description of your activities and include the required information in that narrative. Here are two nonprofits answering this question in different formats. Both are correct. The second example gives IRS more information, but the first example is sufficient.

> It is a guess, so don't worry if the percentages are off in real life.

Example 1: The Corporation will provide tangible assistance to individuals and organizations in the form of funding for or providing actual food, clothing, shelter, medical care, educational assistance, assistive technology and equipment for individuals with handicaps, support for veterans, cultural exchange opportunities, as well as other aid and development programs and projects, especially in but not limited to the United States and devastated, impoverished locations around the world.

1a. Tangible assistance to individuals by providing food, clothing, shelter, medical care, educational assistance, assistive technology and equipment for individuals with handicaps, and support for veterans.
 b. Board members and volunteers conduct this activity.
 c. (Put your city or state or the area you are working in).
 d. 65 percent of our total time is allocated to the activity.
 e. 65 percent of our funding will go to this activity and it will be funded by fundraising events, donations, and grants.
 f. Our exempt purposes include tangible assistance to individuals by providing food, clothing, shelter, medical care, educational assistance, assistive technology and equipment for individuals with handicaps, and support for veterans. By doing these activities, we further our exempt purposes.

2a. Tangible assistance to individuals and organizations in the form of funding.
 b. Board members and volunteers conduct this activity.
 c. (Put your city or state or the area you are working in).
 d. 15 percent of our total time is allocated to the activity.
 e. 15 percent of our funding will go to this activity and it will be funded by fundraising events, donations, and grants.
 f. Our exempt purposes include tangible assistance to individuals and organizations in the form of funding.

By conducting these activities, we further our exempt purpose.

3a. Other aid and development programs and projects, especially in but not limited to the United States and devastated, impoverished locations around the world.
b. Board members and volunteers conduct this activity.
c. (Put your city or state or the area you are working in).
d. 15 percent of our total time is allocated to the activity.
e. 15 percent of our funding will go to this activity and it will be funded by fundraising events, donations, and grants.
f. Our exempt purposes include other aid and development programs and projects, especially in but not limited to the United States and devastated, impoverished locations around the world. By conducting these activities, we further our exempt purposes.

4a. Cultural exchange opportunities
b. Board members and volunteers conduct this activity.
c. Select the countries you will be work with or in.
d. 5 percent of our total time is allocated to the activity.
e. 5 percent of our funding will go to this activity and it will be funded by fundraising events, donations, and grants.
f. Our exempt purposes include cultural exchange opportunities. By conducting this activity, we further our exempt purposes.

Example 2: A narrative format. This one would be included as an attachment because it would not all fit in the box provided. In this case, you would type in, "See Attachment" in the box provided.

The organization was created to foster understanding and collaborations among cultures in the Asia Pacific area and the world with a goal of narrowing the regional development gap, as well as promoting equality, justice, and harmony. The organization will accomplish this mission through research, dialogue, international exchange, and implementing programs that are complementary to The General Conference of the United Nations Educational, Scientific and Cultural Organization (UNESCO) meeting on cultural diversity in Paris from October 3 – 21, 2005.

We share UNESCO's objectives and will implement them in the Asian Pacific region initially, and expand to other areas as we grow as an organization:

a. to protect and promote the diversity of cultural expressions;
b. to create the conditions for cultures to flourish and to freely interact in a mutually beneficial manner;
c. to encourage dialogue among cultures with a view to ensuring wider and balanced cultural exchanges in the world in favor of intercultural respect and a culture of peace;
d. to foster interculturality in order to develop cultural interaction in the spirit of building bridges among peoples;
e. to promote respect for the diversity of cultural expressions and raise awareness of its value at the local, national and international levels;
f. to reaffirm the importance of the link between culture and development for all countries, particularly for developing countries, and to support actions undertaken nationally and internationally to secure recognition of the true value of this link;
g. to give recognition to the distinctive nature of cultural activities, goods and services as vehicles of identity, values and meaning;
h. to reaffirm the sovereign rights of States to maintain, adopt and implement policies and measures that they deem appropriate for the protection and promotion of the diversity of cultural expressions on their territory;

i. to strengthen international cooperation and solidarity in a spirit of partnership with a view, in particular, to enhancing the capacities of developing countries in order to protect and promote the diversity of cultural expressions.

As an organization, we are founded on the principles of dignity and respect, international cooperation and solidarity, sustainable development, encouraging mutual understanding between cultures, and capacity building through free flow of information, cultural exchange, and collaboration.

We will spend our time on collaboration (55%), dialogue (20%), research (15%), and cultural exchange (10%) with a goal of narrowing the regional development gap, as well as promoting equality, justice, and harmony through research, dialogue, international exchange, and implementing programs.

We plan to raise funds through fees charged to attend collaboration conferences (55%), grants (20%), donations (15%), and fundraising events (10%).

By doing all these things that are part of our mission, we further our exempt purposes.

Once you complete the activities description box, you are ready to move on to the rest of the activities questions. These questions include:

Line 2. Enter the 3-character NTEE Code that best describes your activities.

An NTEE code contains three character (a letter and two numbers) that gives a broad category of activities to the organization. You can find the list of NTEE codes on pages 15-26 of the document located at *https://www.irs.gov/pub/irs-tege/p4838.pdf* or you can do an internet search for "NTEE Instructions" and open Form 1023-EZ instructions and go to the back of the instructions for a list of NTEE codes well presented in one place. You can also find a webpage with the codes from A to Y at *https://learn.guidestar.org/help/ntee-codes*

Common NTEE codes include:

> P80: Services to Promote the Independence of Specific Populations
> X20: Christian
> A99: Arts, Culture, and Humanities
> D20: Animal Protection and Welfare
> F20: Alcohol, Drug and Substance Abuse, Dependency Prevention, and Treatment
> I72: Prevention of Child Abuse
> O50: Youth Development Programs

There are many NTEE codes. Check them out to find the one that best fits your organization. We suggest you stay away from the codes that start with the letter Y. They are mutual benefit organization codes and do not qualify for 501(c) (3) public charity status.

If you would like IRS to select the NTEE code, check that box on the application.

Line 3. Do any of your programs limit the provision of goods, services, or funds to a specific individual or group of specific individuals? For example, answer "Yes" if goods, services, or funds are provided only for a particular individual, your members, individuals who work for a particular employer, or graduates of a particular school. If "Yes," explain the limitation and how recipients are selected for each program.

The normal answer is "No."

This part of the application seeks to find out how you are selecting your target group to assist and aims to ferret out any selection process that benefits members or private interests instead of public interest. A good test is whether you know ahead of time the names of the people or organizations you will help. If so, you may not be a 501(c)(3) public charity, but a private foundation instead.

If your nonprofit organization will be helping individuals directly, check "Yes" and describe your programs and how you will carry them out. Make sure to emphasize that your target individuals are from a class of people (such as poor, disabled, homeless, or senior citizens), not specific individuals you can name ahead of time. It is permissible to help specific individuals as long as you do not limit your services to specific people and leave open the opportunity to add others in the future whose names you do not even know yet. If you will be helping individuals only indirectly through other organizations, check "No" and move on.

Line 4. Do any individuals who receive goods, services, or funds through your programs have a family or business relationship with any officer, director, trustee, or with any of your highest compensated employees or highest compensated independent contractors? If "Yes," explain how these related individuals are eligible for goods, services, or funds.

The correct answer is "No."

Line 5. Do you or will you support or oppose candidates in political campaigns in any way? If "Yes," explain.

The correct answer is "No."

Line 6. Do you or will you attempt to influence legislation? If "Yes," explain how you attempt to influence legislation.

The correct answer is "No."

Line 7. Do you or will you publish, own, or have rights in music, literature, tapes, artworks, choreography, scientific discoveries, or other intellectual property? If "Yes," describe who owns or will own any copyrights, patents, or trademarks, whether fees are or will be charged, how the fees are determined, and how any items are or will be produced, distributed, and marketed.

Intellectual property includes patents for inventions; copyrights (for literary and artistic works such as novels, poems, plays, films, musical works, drawings, paintings, photographs, sculptures, architectural designs, performances, recordings, film, and radio or television programs); trade names, trademarks, and service marks (for symbols, names, images, and designs); and formulas, know-how, and trade secrets).

Intellectual property also includes any written materials either published, printed, copied, or displayed on a website online. If you have a slogan or a logo, this is also intellectual property. If you are just starting out and have none of these yet, answer "No."

If you have developed any educational materials, brochures, or websites or any intellectual property from the ones listed above, you must answer "Yes," and give complete details on all items required for this line.

Here is our best guidance based on experience: If you personally have developed intellectual property, keep the rights to that property, but allow the nonprofit to use the materials you developed. Why? Because if you *give* it to the nonprofit and the nonprofit closes, you cannot have it back. You must give it to another nonprofit. If you *loan* it to the nonprofit, or *lease* it to the nonprofit, you still own it and if the nonprofit closes, you still own it and do not have to give it to another nonprofit. This can include books, domains, programs, trademarks, logos, and other items of intellectual property.

Line 8. Do you or will you provide educational information to the general public on budgeting, personal finance, financial literacy, saving and spending practices, the sound use of consumer credit, and/or assist individuals and families with financial problems such as credit card debt and foreclosure by providing them with counseling? If "Yes," explain.

The answer for most organizations is "No." However, if your mission includes these areas, give details of what you will do and services you will provide, if you will charge for your services, what your fees are (if applicable) and how you will determine fees. Also address the areas below required under IRS Code 501 q.

Credit and financial counseling fall under an additional section of IRS Code: Section 501 q. If you want to be a 501(c) (3) organization, your credit and financial services must meet these 501 q rules as well as the normal 501(c) (3) requirements:

Services – Must provide credit counseling services tailored to the specific needs and circumstances of the consumer
Loans – Cannot make loans to debtors unless no fees or interest
Credit Repair – Can only provide incidental services to improve consumer credit records and credit history, and cannot charge a separate fee for such services
Ability to Pay – Cannot refuse services based on ability to pay or ineligibility/unwillingness of consumer to enroll in a debt management plan ("DMP")
Fee Policy – Must charge reasonable fees and provide waivers if consumer is unable to pay

WISCONSIN

- **Board Composition** – Majority of members must represent broad interests of the public; maximum of 49 percent can be employed by organization or benefit from it
- **Ownership** – Cannot own more than 35 percent of an entity that is involved in the credit counseling or similar business
- **Referrals** – Cannot pay for referrals or receive amounts for providing referrals for debt management plans

(From *https://www.irs.gov/charities-non-profits/credit-counseling-legislation-new-criteria-for-exemption* updated June 7, 2019).

Line 9. Do you or will you make grants, loans, or other distributions to organizations? If "Yes," describe the type and purpose of the grants, loans, or distributions, how you select your recipients including submission requirements (such as grant proposals or application forms), and the criteria you use or will use to select recipients. Also describe how you ensure the grants, loans, and other distributions are or will be used for their intended purposes (including whether you require periodic or final reports on the use of funds and any procedures you have if you identify that funds are not being used for their intended purposes). Finally, describe the records you keep with respect to grants, loans, or other distributions you make and identify any recipient organizations and any relationships between you and the recipients. If "No," continue to Line 10.

If you make grants, loans, or distributions to organizations, you need to answer each part of this section and include copies of all forms you use in deciding who is eligible for a loan, grant, or distribution, how much they get, and how you will monitor the funds to make sure they are being used for exempt purposes, and what you will do if you find out that the funds were not used for the intended purpose.

You also need to describe how you will keep records and what reports you will require. If there is a relationship between you and the grantee, you must disclose those details in your explanation.

Here is an acceptable way to answer Line 9 for new organizations just getting started. (you can borrow these words if they apply):

> *We do not offer grants or loans to organizations. Other distributions to organizations assisting us in conducting our mission will be documented with copies of receipts, letters, or other relevant documentation. According to our bylaws, all business including any distributions would have to be approved by the board of directors. The method of approval would be documented. Distributions to organizations have not yet occurred since the incorporation.*

> *We will maintain our financial records on QuickBooks or similar software in accordance with general accounting principles for nonprofit organizations. Cash received is applied to Accounts Receivable Ledger and cash distributed is recorded in the Accounts Payable ledger. Likewise, organizations that receive distributions are required to maintain general accounting records and are required to report on a regular/monthly basis as to how, when, and where funds are applied. If funds are not used for the intended purposes, we will discontinue all financial transactions with the organization and have nothing further to do with them.*

If you answered "Yes" to Line 9, you have a few additional questions to answer.

Line 9a. Do you or will you make grants, loans, or other distributions to organizations that are not recognized by the IRS as tax exempt under section 501(c) (3)? If "Yes," name and/or describe the non-section 501(c) (3) organizations to whom you do or will make distributions and explain how these distributions further your exempt purposes.

Answer "No" if you can. Most organizations in the United States will have 501(c) (3) status. If you are distributing to an organization in the USA that does not have tax-exempt status, explain why you are making distributions to them, and how that helps you accomplish your tax-exempt mission.

If you are donating or making distributions to organizations outside the United States, they will not have 501(c) (3) tax-exempt status. In that case, you might add this to the narrative box:

> *It is our intent that if we distribute through organizations, that they would be 501(c) (3) eligible if they were located in the United States, however Revenue Ruling 68-489, 1968-2 C.B. 210 states that an organization will not jeopardize its exemption under Section 501(c) (3) of the code, even though it distributes funds to nonexempt organizations, provided it retains control and discretion over use of the funds for Section 501(c) (3) purposes.*

> *We do not offer or provide loans or grants to other organizations. Any distributions to other organizations will only include funds necessary to carry out our mission as it has been described in Part IV, Line 1 of this application. These distributions would be funds donated to organizations which would be capable of addressing the issues we address in a more timely and effective manner than we would be able to at the given time. The board of directors will conduct due diligence and maintain control of any funds contributed to*

any organization regardless of their exempt status and will comply with all applicable laws and guidelines to maintain and further our exempt status.

Line 9b. Do you or will you make grants, loans, or other distributions to foreign organizations? If "Yes," name each foreign organization (if not already provided), the country and region within each country in which each foreign organization operates, any relationship you have with each foreign organization, and whether the foreign organization accepts contributions earmarked for a specific country or organization (if so, specify which countries or organizations). If "No," continue to Line 10.

If you are a brand new organization that plans to operate internationally, here is an answer IRS will accept. Feel free to change it to fit the specifics of your organization:

Currently, we have no financial recipient organizations and plan to administer our programs through efforts of board members and volunteers. We will develop relationships over time. Any foreign organization we work with will not accept contributions earmarked for a specific country or organization.

We do not offer or provide grants or loans to any foreign or domestic organizations. If we decide a contribution or distribution is necessary to fulfill our mission and our duty to further our exempt status, we will contribute to foreign or domestic organizations at the discretion of the board of directors. If we decide to contribute to an organization, we will stipulate how the funds shall be used and require the recipient to provide us with detailed records and financial proof of how the funds were utilized.

If you are giving loans or grants, give the name of the organization(s), the country and the region within the country (a specific city, or compass direction such as north, south, east, or west or commonly known region), any relationship you have with the organization (such as shared board members or relatives), and whether the foreign organization accepts contributions earmarked for a specific country or organization.

Line 9c. Do your contributors know that you have ultimate authority to use contributions made to you at your discretion for purposes consistent with your exempt purposes? If "Yes," describe how you relay this information to contributors.

The answer is: *We will tell them specifically during direct contact and will have it printed on our donation receipts.*

Line 9d. Do you or will you make pre-grant inquiries about the recipient organization? If "Yes," describe these inquiries, including whether you inquire about the recipient's financial status, its tax-exempt status under the Internal Revenue Code, its ability to accomplish the purpose for which the resources are provided, and other relevant information.

Here is a good answer:

We do not offer or provide grants to any individuals or organizations. But for any contributions made by the Corporation to any organization, we take into consideration the tax exempt status based on whether it is exempt (or it would be exempt under Internal Revenue Code if located in the United States), overall financial standing of the recipient, and we inquire about any reasonably available historical information about the recipient identity and integrity, the available postal, email, and website addresses and phone number of each place of business of the recipient, and a statement of general purpose of the recipient, including a detailed report of the recipient projects and goals.

Line 9e. Do you or will you use any additional procedures to ensure that your distributions to foreign organizations are used in furtherance of your exempt purposes? If "Yes," describe these procedures, including periodic reporting requirements, auditing grantees, site visits by your employees or compliance checks by impartial experts, etc., to verify that grant funds are being used appropriately.

Here is a good answer:

We do not distribute to any organization unless we have a board member or other responsible representative in that country overseeing distribution of the funds until the integrity of a local organization has been established. The board of directors will maintain control of any funds contributed to any organization and will comply with all applicable laws and guidelines.

Line 9f. Do you share board members or other key personnel with the recipient organization(s)? If "Yes," identify the relationships.

If you are giving funds to another organization, disclose any shared board members between the two organizations.

Line 9g. When you make grants, loans, or other distributions to foreign organizations, will you check the OFAC List of Specially Designated Nationals and Blocked Persons for names of individuals and entities with whom you are dealing to determine if they are included on the list? Describe any other practices you will engage in to ensure that foreign expenditures or grants are not diverted to support terrorism or other non-charitable activities. Mark "Yes," and then here is a good written answer to type in the box:

> *Although adherence and compliance with the U. S. Department of the Treasury publication the Voluntary Best Practices for U. S. Based Charities is not mandatory, we willfully and voluntarily recognize and put into practice these guidelines and suggestions to reduce, develop, reevaluate, and strengthen a risk based approach to guard against the threat of diversion of charitable funds or exploitation of charitable activity by terrorist organizations and their support networks. We also comply and put into practice the federal guidelines, suggestions, laws, and limitations set forth by preexisting U. S. legal requirements related to combating terrorist financing, which include, but are not limited to, various sanctions programs administered by the Office of Foreign Assets Control OFAC in regard to our foreign activities.*

Line 9h. Will you comply with all United States statutes, executive orders, and regulations that restrict or prohibit U.S. persons from engaging in transactions and dealings with designated countries, entities, or individuals, or otherwise engaging in activities in violation of economic sanctions administered by OFAC?

The correct answer is "Yes."

Line 9i. Will you acquire from OFAC the appropriate license and registration where necessary?

The correct answer is "Yes."

Line 10. Do you or will you operate in a foreign country or countries? If "Yes," name each foreign country and region within each country in which you do or will operate and describe your operations in each one. If "No," continue to Line 11.

If you answer "Yes," put this information in the box:

> *We will begin operations in (name the country and region or city, such as Andhra Pradesh, India or all regions of Eswatini) and expand to other countries as the organization grows over time.*

By stating here that you will expand to other countries as the organization grows, you are not limiting yourself to just the place you are starting. Who knows where you might operate ten years down the road? Get approved worldwide now so you can operate where you want to later.

If you answered "Yes," you have other questions to answer.

Line 10a. When you conduct activities in foreign countries, will you check the OFAC List of Specially Designated Nationals and Blocked Persons for names of individuals and entities with whom you are dealing to determine if they are included on the list? Describe any other practices you will engage in to ensure that foreign expenditures or grants are not diverted to support terrorism or other non-charitable activities.

Answer "Yes," and here is a good answer to type in the box:

We generally do not distribute to any organization unless we have a board member or other responsible representative in that country overseeing distribution of the funds until the integrity of a local organization has been established. The board of directors will maintain control of any funds contributed to any organization and will comply with all applicable laws and guidelines. Although adherence and compliance with the U. S. Department of the Treasury publication, "Voluntary Best Practices of U. S. Based Charities" is not mandatory, we willfully and voluntarily recognize and put into practice these guidelines and suggestions to reduce, develop, re-evaluate, and strengthen a risk-based approach to guard against the threat of diversion of charitable funds or exploitation of charitable activity by terrorist organizations and their support networks.

Line 10b. Will you comply with all United States statutes, executive orders, and regulations that restrict or prohibit U.S. persons from engaging in transactions and dealings with designated countries, entities, or individuals, or otherwise engaging in activities in violation of economic sanctions administered by OFAC?

The correct answer is "Yes."

Line 10c. Will you acquire from OFAC the appropriate license and registration where necessary?

The correct answer is "Yes."

Line 11. Are you a sponsoring organization that maintains one or more donor advised funds? If yes, please provide a complete description of your program, including the specific advice that such donors may provide. Describe in detail the control you maintain (or will maintain) over the use of the funds.

The simplest answer you can give is "No." A donor advised fund is set up by a sponsoring organization such as Vanguard or Fidelity or other corporation. Donors can set up an account, put stock or money or other valuables in the account, and get an immediate tax deduction even though they have not specified where the money is to go. The person who set up the giving account cannot have the money back; he or she must give it away to a 501(c) organization. Over time, the donor selects organizations to get funds. When you get a check from a Fidelity giving account, the check is drawn on Fidelity's bank, but the memo will include who the donor is that advised Fidelity to send the check. One of our board advisors for Pasture Valley Children Missions has a donor advised account with Fidelity. Periodically, he authorizes donations for different programs he wants to donate to, and Fidelity sends out the check. The board advisor's name is on the memo as the person who authorized the funds, but the check is from Fidelity.

Line 12. Do you or will you operate a school? If "Yes," complete Schedule B.

Mark "No" if you are not a school. Mark "Yes" if you are a school, then click on Schedule B. Guidance for Schedule B is in Chapter 25.

Line 13. Is your principal purpose or function to provide hospital or medical care? If "Yes," complete Schedule C.

Mark "No" if you are not providing medical care. Mark "Yes" if you are, then click on Schedule C. Guidance for Schedule C is in Chapter 26.

Line 14. Do you or will you provide low-income housing? If "Yes," complete Schedule F.

Mark "No" if you are not providing low-income housing. Mark "Yes" if you are, then click on Schedule F. Guidance for Schedule F is in Chapter 29.

Line 15. Do you or will you provide scholarships, fellowships, educational loans, or other educational grants to individuals, including grants for travel, study, or other similar purposes? If "Yes," complete Schedule H - Section I.

Mark "No" if you are not providing educational funds for scholarships, fellowships, loans or grants. Mark "Yes" if you are, then click on Schedule H – Section I. Guidance for Schedule H is in Chapter 31.

Line 16. Check any of the following fundraising activities that you will undertake (check all that apply).

If you plan to raise funds, tell IRS how you plan to do that. Check the boxes that apply to your plans. If you check "Other (describe)," put some explanation of your plans such as hosting fundraising events, charity golf tournaments, etc.

If you do not plan to raise funds, check the box at the end of Line 16 that says, "We will not engage in fundraising activities."

Line 17. Do you or will you engage in fundraising activities for other organizations? If "Yes," describe these arrangements, including the names or descriptions of the organizations for which you raise funds.

Mark "No" if you do not plan to raise funds for other organizations. Mark "Yes" if you do and explain what you will do, for what organizations (if you know yet), and if there will be a split of the funds between the two organizations, any fees charged or deducted, or if you will just raise funds and give it to the other organization(s) as part of your tax-exempt mission.

CHAPTER 19

PART V

COMPENSATION AND OTHER FINANCIAL ARRANGEMENTS

"How wonderful it is that no one need wait a single moment before starting to improve the world."

—Anne Frank

POSSIBLE CONFLICTS OF INTEREST

This section of your application is designed to disclose any conflicts of interest, personal profit to organization officials (or their friends, business associates, or family members), and undue influence because of relationships, contracts, and mingled loyalties between organizations. If you are a new organization just beginning operations, this section will be easy and fast to complete because chances are you that will not have any of these issues to disclose.

If you are a new organization just beginning operations, this section will be easy and fast to complete

Line 1. Do you or will you compensate officers, directors, or trustees, or do or will you have highest compensated employees, or highest compensated independent contractors? If "No," continue to Line 2.

If you answered "No," go to Line 2. If you answered "Yes," you must answer the following questions.

In establishing compensation for your officers, directors, trustees, highest compensated employees, and highest compensated independent contractors:

Line 1a. Do or will the individuals that approve compensation arrangements follow a conflict of interest policy?

The correct answer is "Yes."

Line 1b. Do or will you approve compensation arrangements in advance of paying compensation?

The correct answer is "Yes."

Line 1c. Do or will you document in writing the date and terms of approved compensation arrangements?

The correct answer is "Yes."

Line 1d. Do or will you record in writing the decision made by each individual who decided or voted on compensation arrangements?

The correct answer is "Yes."

Line 1e. Do or will you approve compensation arrangements based on information about compensation paid by similarly situated taxable or tax-exempt organizations for similar services, current compensation surveys compiled by independent firms, or actual written offers from similarly situated organizations?

You can't just pay any amount you want. You must make sure the compensation is fair, comparable to other organizations of similar size, mission, and geographic region, and that the amount paid is equal to the work done for the money. Paying $175,000 a year for 10 hours work a week wouldn't be equal to the work done for the money. However, Paying $75,000 a year for a well-qualified, experienced Executive Director working 40 to 50 hours per week would be considered fair compensation if the job responsibilities were comparable to other people in the same job in corporations of similar size and mission who were making the same amount or more. You must do some salary research before hiring people to run your organization. As long as the compensation is equal to or less than similar organizations, there is no problem.

The correct answer to this question is "Yes."

Line 1f. Do or will you record in writing both the information on which you relied to base your decision and its source?

The correct answer is "Yes."

Line 1g. Do or will you have any other practices you use to set reasonable compensation? If "Yes," describe these practices.

Answer "Yes" and type in the box, "*We will use job descriptions for each position that includes tasks to be performed, working hours, qualifications for the positions, and salary as determined by the board after analyzing our financial capacities and researching compensation by similar organizations for similar positions.*"

Line 2. Have you adopted a conflict of interest policy consistent with the sample conflict of interest policy in Appendix A to the instructions? If you are a hospital, answer "Yes" if your conflict of interest policy includes provisions consistent with the additional healthcare related provisions in the sample document. If "No," describe the procedures you will follow to ensure that persons who have a conflict of interest will not have influence over setting their own compensation or regarding business deals with themselves.

The correct answer is "Yes."

Line 3. Do you or will you compensate any of your officers, directors, trustees, highest compensated employees, and highest compensated independent contractors through non-fixed payments, such as discretionary bonuses or revenue-based payments? If "Yes," describe all non-fixed compensation arrangements, including how the amounts are determined, who is eligible for such arrangements, whether you place a limitation on total compensation, and how you determine or will determine that you pay no more than reasonable compensation for services.

If you answer "Yes" to this item, you have waved a huge red flag, and your tax-exempt status is not likely to be approved. If you are basing compensation on performance, percentages, revenue or bonuses, you are using non-fixed payments, and IRS looks for corruption and sees this as a way to spread the profits around to insiders.

The correct answer is "No."

Line 4. Do you or will you purchase or sell any goods, services, or assets from or to: (i) any of your officers, directors, or trustees; (ii) any family of any of your officers, directors, or trustees; (iii) any organizations in which any of your officers,

directors, or trustees are also officers, directors, or trustees, or in which any individual officer, director, or trustee owns more than a 35% interest; (iv) your highest compensated employees; or (v) your highest compensated independent contractors? If "Yes," describe any such transactions that you made or intend to make, with whom you make or will make such transactions, how the terms are or will be negotiated at arm's length, and how you determine you pay no more than fair market value or you are paid at least fair market value.

Another big red flag here if you answer "Yes." If you do purchase any goods, services, or assets from insiders, make sure you explain it well in the narrative box and give the IRS agent enough details to be comfortable with the business arrangement. If you have a contract, add a copy to the uploaded document at the end of the application.

Line 5. Do you or will you have any leases, contracts, loans, or other agreements with: (i) your officers, directors, or trustees; (ii) any family of any of your officers, directors, or trustees; (iii) any organizations in which any of your officers, directors, or trustees are also officers, directors, or trustees, or in which any individual officer, director, or trustee owns more than a 35% interest; (iv) your highest compensated employees; or (v) your highest compensated independent contractors? If "Yes," describe any written or oral arrangements that you made or intend to make, with whom you have or will have such arrangements, how the terms are or will be negotiated at arm's length, and how you determine you pay no more than fair market value or you are paid at least fair market value.

The easiest answer is "No." However, that may not be the case. This question is trying to uncover any undue influence, or conflicts of interest, of officials who might also have influence or ownership (35% or more) in another organization that your organization will do business with. Answering "Yes" does not necessarily throw up a red flag unless the remuneration is more than is customary for the services or facilities in question. Remember to provide copies of all documents and include an in-depth explanation in the narrative box. If there is not enough room, type in "See Attached," and include your explanation in the attachment along with the other documents you must submit.

Line 6. Do you or will you contract with another organization to develop, build, market, or finance your facilities? If "Yes," describe each facility, the role of the other organization, and any business or family relationship between the organization and your officers, directors, or trustees. Explain how that entity is selected, how the terms of any contract(s) are negotiated at arm's length, and how you determine you will pay no more than fair market value for services.

The simplest answer is "No." If that is not the case, then you must explain the details of your plans and how you will ensure that you are not paying more than the going rate for the services provided. If you are building a facility at some point in the future, you might say something like:

> *If we cannot locate a suitable facility to remodel, we will build a 32-unit apartment building of one-bedroom units to house homeless people for up to one year while they get on their feet. We will accept bids from no less than five local or regional contractors of good reputation and experience, and the board will determine which to hire. None of the contractors will be related to the board or have any other dealings with the organization. We will determine fair market value from price-per-square foot guidance for our area, as well as local real estate values for similar facilities.*

Line 7. Does or will someone other than your own employees or volunteers manage your activities or facilities? If "Yes," describe the activities or facilities that will be managed by others, the names of the persons or organizations that manage or will manage your activities or facilities, and any business or family relationship between the organization and your officers, directors, or trustees. Explain how these managers were or will be selected, how the terms of any contracts or other agreements were or will be negotiated, and how you determine you will pay no more than fair market value for services.

The easiest answer to this question is "No." If your particulars require you to answer otherwise, then give IRS the details of your plans. For example, if you are starting a charter school, you might hire outside help for back-of-the-house functions such as providing lunches, cleaning services, or accounting. In those cases, it is customary to have a written service contract with fees, services to be provided, the length of time the services are contracted for, what constitutes a breach of contract, and the penalty for the breach. If you already have a contract, then attach a copy to the application. If not, explain how you will select the contractor, how you will make sure they are not charging too much, and be sure to either state that there are no family or business relationships, or if there are, the nature of the relationships. You need to convince IRS that family or business relationships were the best choices for the organization because the fees were less and the services better than the competition.

Line 8. Do you participate in any joint ventures, including partnerships or limited liability companies treated as partnerships, in which you share profits and losses with partners? If "Yes," state your ownership percentage in each joint venture, list your investment in each joint venture, describe the tax status of other participants in each joint venture (including whether they are section 501(c) (3) organizations), describe the activities of each joint venture, describe how you exercise control over the activities of each joint venture, and describe how each joint venture furthers your exempt purposes.

The BEST answer is "NO!"

This item seeks to establish whether your tax-exempt organization plans to join forces for purposes of creating profit, with other individuals or organizations that are not 501(c) (3) approved. IRS defines a joint venture as:

> *"a legal agreement in which the persons*
> *jointly undertake a transaction*
> *for mutual profit. Generally, each person*
> *contributes assets and shares risks.*
> *Like a partnership, a joint venture can involve*
> *any kind of business transaction*
> *and the persons involved can be individuals,*
> *companies, or corporations."*

A nonprofit that Kitty founded (*Pasture Valley Children Missions*, EIN 35-2468924) entered a joint venture with a local pharmacy to provide a market for jewelry made by women in Swaziland through the Bambanani Project. The agreement called for a 20% commission (the pharmacy's standard commission) on all items sold. This is the type of agreement that would need to be disclosed and explained if known or planned at the time of application.

As it turned out, no commission was actually ever charged. The pharmacy donated the commission to the organization instead.

The same type of agreement was made with another organization to market the jewelry but was not an issue because the second organization was also a tax-exempt organization. You can work with other nonprofit entities and share benefits between organizations in any way you see fit as long as all profits go to the tax-exempt missions of the organizations.

This is a tricky area, and we highly recommend you talk with IRS about it if you have any joint ventures in force or planned with organizations that are not tax exempt.

FINANCIAL REPORT

3.456
2.589
1.258
4.896

3.45   2.58   6.58   12.3

8.52   6.47
.58   6.02
56   7.43

CHAPTER 20

PART VI

FINANCIAL DATA

*"The question isn't who is going to let me;
It's who is going to stop me."*

—Ayn Rand

THE MONEY

This section may seem difficult or tricky, but it does not have to be. IRS wants to know what has occurred financially to date with your organization, and/or what you expect to happen in the near future (the next few years). If you are a brand-new organization that has had nothing but minimal financial support or transactions, then this part is very easy to complete. Just remember that what you put in this section must match the rest of the application including any narrative you provided in answer to any other question. IRS requires financial information for three years if you are less than a year old (this year, next year, and the year after), and up to four years if you are more than one year old (this year, and whatever combination of years past and future produces four years of information). If you have existed for five or more years without filing for 501(c) (3) status, complete financial information for the past five years and make sure it matches your tax returns for the past five years.

Line 1. Select the option that best describes you to determine the years of revenues and expenses you need to provide.

Select the choice of the organization being in operation for less than one year, more than one year but less than five years, or five or more years. You can calculate from the date of incorporation.

> **NOTE:** You could include prior years of operation if you began operations before you incorporated, but your official start date is the date of incorporation with the state. It may be simpler to include from date of incorporation forward if you did not file nonprofit tax returns for those prior years before you incorporated.

EXAMPLE OF FINANCIAL DATA IF YOU ARE NEW AND HAVE NO IDEA WHAT TO ENTER ON THIS FORM (Line-by-line coverage of this form appears in the next section of this chapter, but if you just want to get done, here is a place to start):

If you are a brand new organization, have no revenues yet, have no clue what your income or expenses will be, and think they will be under $10,000, here is an example of how you might fill in the financial data form:

1. For dates:
    Current year: 01/01 and current year to 12/31 and current year.
    Column 2: 01/01/next year to 12/31/next year
    Column 3: 01/01/year after next to 12/31/year after next

2. Revenues: Lines 1 (or Line 9 if you have service revenue such as day care center payments from parents, or tuition fees from martial arts classes, etc.), 8, 10, and 13:

Column 1 for all four lines: 5,000
Column 2 for all four lines: 7,000
Column 3 for all four lines: 9,000

3. Expenses: Lines 23 and 24
   Column 1: 4,500
   Column 2: 6,500
   Column 3: 8,500

4. Narrative description for Line 25:
   Current year: $1,000 filing and set up fees, $3,500 program services
   Next year: $6,500 program services
   Year after next: $8,500 program services

Yes, feel free to borrow these numbers (or adjust them to fit) if they make sense to your organization. You're welcome!

Financial Data Line-by-Line:

If you have been in existence less than one year, this is going to be so easy! You get to make the whole thing up for three years, giving it your best effort to determine the most likely income and expenses. So, what if you don't know for sure? Give it your best shot. Start somewhere and think it through. Don't stress out over it. Just do it! No penalty for being wrong, but be as accurate as you can, knowing full well you won't know the real numbers until after the fact. IRS knows it is not accurate, you know it is not accurate, but they make you do it anyway. So just do it.

YOU CAN DO THIS!

The financial part of this application has caused more anxiety than probably any other section. RELAX! It's just paperwork, one line at a time, so let's get started:

WISCONSIN

Line 1: Gifts, Grants, and Contributions Received (do not include unusual gifts)

Unusual grants are unexpected large sums received from disinterested parties. Because the amount is large, it can affect your organization's classification as a public charity which must be supported primarily by the general public. For this reason, unusual grants like this are reported further down on the form on Line 12.

On line 1, you report gifts, grants, and contributions (including donations) from various sources that help you accomplish your tax-exempt purpose. You also report government units helping you that provide services or facilities to the general public (as opposed to a specific group). If you receive revenue to complete a program or function for the general public (for example, if your organization is hired by someone or an organization), report it on this line. However, if you sell tickets to the general public as opposed to being hired for a fee to perform, that income goes on Line 9, Gross Receipts. If you are not sure which line to put the income on, contact IRS and ask before filling out the form.

Line 2: Membership Fees Received

Most charitable nonprofits do not have membership fees because they do not have members. Having board members is not the same as having memberships; do not confuse the concepts. If you do have members and you charge a membership fee to support the organization, put the total of the fees on this line. Do not include fees charged to members for anything except membership. Any other fees paid (such as for admission, merchandise, services, or use of facilities) are gross receipts, not membership fees, and get reported on Line 9.

Line 3: Gross Investment Income

Any income received from any investment (loans, rents, royalties, dividends, interest, etc.) is entered here.

Line 4: Net Unrelated Business Income

Does the nonprofit organization have any income from unrelated business activity? Any income of which less than 85% of the labor was not completed by volunteers? Any income that did not have anything to do with your exempt purpose? You report it on line 4. Contact IRS or see Publication 598 (specifically Chapter 4) if you need more information on this line to figure the unrelated business income. You can access it at *htttps://www.irs.gov/pub/irs-pdf/p598.pdf*

Line 5: Taxes Levied for Your Benefit

If the public paid any taxes on your behalf, include the amount collected here.

Line 6: Value of Services or Facilities Furnished by a Government Unit Without Charge (not including the value of services generally furnished to the public without charge)

Use the fair market value that would be charged for an organization that is not tax exempt.

Line 7: Any Revenue Not Otherwise Listed Above or on Lines 9 - 12 below. (Attach an itemized list)

In our opinions, this line should have come AFTER line 12 because you have to complete lines 9 - 12 before you can answer this one. If you have other forms of income that do not fit into one of the other categories, put them here. Itemize them and give a brief description in the narrative box provided at the bottom of the form on Line 25 (less brief if you think IRS needs more details to avoid sending you a letter asking for more information). If in doubt, contact IRS and ask before entering it here.

Line 8: Total of lines 1 through 7

This form automatically calculates the total for you.

Line 9: Gross receipts from admissions, merchandise sold or services performed, or furnishing of facilities in any activity that is related to your exempt purposes (provide an itemized list in the text box that follows this table)

Do not include amounts you have already included on other lines of this form. You only want to count the amounts once. If you received funds for the use of facilities that were not for the direct benefit of the general public, list them here. You must itemize and include what government agency paid you, the purpose of the payment, and the amount. If in doubt, contact IRS and see Publication 598 before filling out this line. You can access this publication at *https://www.irs.gov/pub/irs-pdf/p598.pdf*

Here is IRS guidance on this line:

> *Enter income from activities that you conduct to further your exempt purposes (excluding amounts listed on other lines). Also, include as gross receipts the income from activities conducted:*
>
> - *Intermittently (not regularly carried on), such as an occasional auction;*
> - *With substantially all (at least 85%) volunteer labor, such as a car wash;*

- *For the convenience of members, students, patients, officers, or employees, such as a parking lot for a school's students and employees; or*
- *With substantially all contributed merchandise, such as a thrift store.*

Line 10: Total of lines 8 and 9

This form automatically calculates the total for you.

Line 11: Net Gain or Loss on the Sale of Capital Assets

IRS guidance on this item is:

Enter any net gain or loss on the sale of capital assets. Provide an itemized list by asset category (for example, real estate or securities) showing gross sales, cost or other basis/sales expenses, and gain or loss by asset category in line 25.

If this line applies to your organization and if desired, you can create a form similar to this one and attach it to the application with all the other required documents. In that case, in the box for Line 25, write, "See Statement of Revenues and Expenses for Line 11" in attachments.

Statement of Revenues and Expenses
Line 11. Net Gain or (Loss)

		Categories		
		(A) Real Estate	(B) Securities	(C) Other
1.	Gross sales price of assets (other than inventory) by category.			
2.	**Less:** Cost or other basis and sales expenses.			
3.	Gain or (loss). Subtract line 2 from line 1.			
4.	Net gain or (loss) - Add line 3 of columns (A), (B), and (C). Enter here and on Form 1023, Part VI, Statement of Revenues and Expenses, line 11.			

If this line applies to your organization, put the total amounts for each category (not an itemized list). Create this format as best you can to include all required information. No actual form exists, we just created this one from an IRS example so you would not have to create one.

Line 12: Unusual Grants

Did you unexpectedly receive a large grant from a disinterested party? This is where you record it. You must also provide an itemized list of the unusual grants in the box for Line 25.

Line 13: Total Revenue. (add lines 10 through12)

This form automatically calculates the total for you.

That takes care of the revenues. Now we deal with the expenses.

Line 14: Fundraising Expenses

What are you spending (or plan to spend) on fundraising? If you hire a professional fundraiser, you must disclose the amount paid here as well. Attach a copy of the fundraising contract to the application if you have one. Fundraising income should be included as part of the amount you listed on Line 1. This line is to show how much you spent to raise funds.

Line 15: Contributions, gifts, grants, and similar amounts paid out (provide an itemized list below)

If you paid out or plan to pay out funds to people or organizations as part of your mission, then IRS needs the details. Who received the funds? How much? What for? If disclosing the name of the individual receiving the payout violates privacy provisions (such as names of those who receive scholarships), then lump the totals together and list them by program or category instead of by person. If you are not paying out directly to individuals or organizations, but instead providing goods or services to individuals or organizations, then don't include the amounts here; include them as program services on Line 23. You provide the itemized list in the box for Line 25. If you need more room, write "Line 15: See Attached" in the box for Line 25 and attach the list with the other documents you submit with the application.

Line 16: Disbursements to or for the benefit of members (provide an itemized list below)

If you disbursed funds to members of your organization, a full disclosure of who, how much, and why is required. Do not include any amount already included in Line 15. Make sure to explain this item completely. Exempt organizations under Section 501(c) (3) exist to benefit the public, not their members, so this area can be a little tricky. If in doubt, contact IRS and talk with them about your specifics before filling out this line. Provide your explanation in the box for Line 25.

Line 17: Compensation of officers, directors, and trustees

Enter the totals for all columns. You normally do not compensate board members. Reimbursing out-of-pocket expenses that board members incur while on organization business is not considered compensation.

Line 18: Other salary and wages

Do you have any employees who are not officers, directors, or trustees? Enter the totals paid to them (or planned in the future) in all columns. If you don't know, don't have funds to pay anyone, and have no idea how much you will be able to pay, just leave it blank. You can add employees when funds are available by voting on hiring at any board meeting, at any time in the future, when you are financially able to fund hiring an employee. Then you report the amounts paid to employees on your Form 990-series tax returns.

Line 19: Interest expense

How much interest did you pay, if any? Do not include mortgage interest if it is being reported as part of occupancy expense on Line 20.

Line 20: Occupancy (rent, utilities, etc.)

Utilities, mortgage interest, real estate taxes, janitorial services, rent, electricity, heat, etc. This includes all facilities for which you pay these expenses to complete your exempt purpose.

Line 21: Depreciation and Depletion

These are calculated the same way they would be in a for-profit organization; the same rules apply. If in doubt, contact IRS and ask before filling in this line.

Line 22: Professional Fees

Accounting, consulting, legal counsel, contract management, and other fees paid to people or organizations who are not your employees. Do not include professional fundraising fees here that you have already reported on Line 14. Independent contractor fees would be reported on this line. If you paid someone or a business to help you prepare and file your documents for incorporation and 501(c)(3) application, those would be professional fees. You can also include contractors who set up websites and provide other professional services for hire, or you can list those fees paid on line 23, but you have to itemize line 23, so it is easier to include them here.

Line 23: Any expense not otherwise classified, such as program services (provide an itemized list below)

If you have expenses that were not included elsewhere on the form, combine the totals here, and make an itemized list in the box for Line 25. Examples of expenses that may not be included above could be the IRS filing fee for the Form 1023, the cost of this book, postage, telephone service (if not included in occupancy above), vehicle expenses, insurance payments, website fees if not claimed on Line 22, even bank charges can be included here. This is the catch-all line very much like the one at the end of Schedule C of Form 1040 for business owners. This is where you list the cost to run specific programs (program service fees). For example, suppose your tax-exempt purpose is to run an afterschool program for at-risk kids. Your program services fees would include the cost of snacks, sports equipment, materials, and anything else you need to operate the program. You can lump them together as program service fees in the box for line 25, or you can break them down into snacks, sports equipment, etc. Your choice.

Line 24: Total Expenses (Add Lines 14 -23)

This form automatically calculates the total for you.

B. Balance Sheet (for your most recently completed tax year)

A balance sheet is a financial statement that states the net worth of a business on a specific date. It includes the assets and the liabilities.

IRS wants to know the net worth as of the last day of the most recently completed fiscal year. If your tax year ends in December, then the date IRS wants to know about is December 31 of last year. This is great news for a new nonprofit that did not exist on December 31 last year. Every line gets a zero, and you are ready to move on.

If your organization did exist as of the last day of your most recently completed fiscal year, then the information you provide should reflect the status as of that last day of the fiscal year.

ASSETS

Line 1: Cash

Combine all short-term assets (less than one year until maturity) and put in the total. This includes cash, petty cash, money in checking and savings accounts, money markets, certificates of deposit, treasury bills, etc.

Line 2: Accounts receivable, net

Unpaid accounts that you expect to collect from sales or services, minus any reserve for bad debts. Most nonprofits have no accounts receivable.

Line 3: Inventories

What do you have on hand that you bought, or made, and are either going to use or sell in the future? What is the inventory worth after you subtract the cost to produce or acquire it? Most nonprofits have no inventory.

Line 4. Bonds and notes receivable (provide an itemized list below)

This item is for bonds or notes your organization issued that you expect to be repaid. The itemized list in the box for Line 19 needs to include the borrower's name, what the form of the obligation is and a description, the rate of return, when it is due, and how much is due. Most organizations do not have Bonds and Notes Receivable.

Line 5: Corporate stocks (provide an itemized list below)

What is the fair market value of stocks your organization holds? The itemized list in the box for Line 19 should include any stocks from closely-held corporations (those companies in which although the public owns some stock, most of it is held by a few people who have no plans to sell it). Include the name of the company, its capital structure, how many shares are held, and the fair market value. For stock listed on an exchange or sold in sufficient quantities over the counter to make it liquid, you must include the name of the company, the exchange, identify the stock and number of shares, and the fair market value. Most new nonprofits do not have any corporate stock, but sometimes someone donates stock to help the organization.

Line 6: Loans receivable (provide an itemized list below)

If your organization made loans, either uncollateralized or mortgage loans, in the box for Line 19, you must list each loan separately and who the loans were made to, the amounts, purpose, interest rates, and terms for how the loans are being paid back. Total all the loans and put that amount on Line 6. Most new nonprofits do not have any loans receivable.

Line 7: Other investments (provide an itemized list below)

This is where you list items such as government securities or properties held for investment. List them separately in the box for Line 19 and give the value of each. Most new nonprofits do not have investments.

Line 8: Depreciable assets (provide an itemized list below)

This is where you list items, equipment, or buildings not held for investment. In the box for Line 19, be sure to include the cost basis of the item in the itemized list. The cost basis is the original cost minus depreciation.

Line 9: Land

This is where you list the value of land that the organization owns that is not for investment.

Line 10: Other assets (provide an itemized list below)

Anything else the organization owns, including patents and intellectual property, gets a book value assigned and is listed here. Itemize in the box for Line 19.

Line 11: Total Assets (Add lines 1 through 10)

This form automatically calculates the total for you.

LIABILITIES

Line 12: Accounts Payable

Include bills that need to be paid or are payable but not yet due. For example, suppliers, salaries, accumulated payroll taxes, and interest.

Line 13: Contributions, gifts, grants, etc. payable

What commitments have you made that you have not yet paid for? For example, are you obligated to a scholarship but have not written the check? This category includes commitments to individuals and organizations.

Line 14: Mortgages and notes payable (provide an itemized list below)

What are the balances due for notes and mortgages at the end of the current tax year/period? On the itemized list in the box for Line 19, show each note or mortgage, the lender, purpose, repayment terms, interest rate, and the original amount of the loan.

Line 15: Other liabilities (provide an itemized list below)

If the organization owes anything else, put it here and list it in the box for Line 19 with sufficient detail to satisfy the IRS agent's curiosity.

Line 16: Total Liabilities (Add lines 12 through 15)

This form automatically calculates the total for you.

FUND BALANCES OR NET ASSETS

Line 17: Total Fund Balances or Net Assets

Enter your total fund balances (if you use fund accounting) or net assets (if you don't).

Line 18: Total Liabilities and Fund Balances or Net Assets (Add lines 16 and 17)

This form automatically calculates the total for you.

Line 19: Itemized financial data

Use this box to give details of any of the questions from 1 through 18 of the balance sheet.

WHEW! GLAD THAT IS DONE!

Go have a cup of coffee or a latte or a sweet tea and relax. You earned it!

CHAPTER 21

PART VII

FOUNDATION CLASSIFICATION

*"When you have confidence,
you can have a lot of fun. And when you have fun,
you can do amazing things."*

—Joe Namath

Part VII is designed to classify you as an organization that is either a private foundation or a public charity. Public charity classification is a more favorable tax status than private foundation classification. If you are a private foundation, this part will further determine whether you are a private operating foundation.

WHY YOU ARE A PUBLIC CHARITY

Part VII is where you establish yourself as a public charity instead of a private foundation. For foundations, donations are only deductible up to 30% of adjusted gross income (with a few limited exceptions); public charity donations are deductible up to 60% of adjusted gross income.

At the beginning of this book, we looked at why you would be a public charity instead of a private foundation. In brief, your source of income in a private foundation does not come from the public, while a public charity's revenues do. To be a public charity, you must be a church, school, hospital, government unit, be testing for public safety, receive most of your support from the general public, or support other organizations that are public charities. Otherwise, you are a private foundation.

For this next section of the form, you need to decide which of the options applies to your organization. If you are a public charity that is not a school, church, hospital, or research facility, you will fall into one of the first two categories: The first choice (mostly supported by donations and fundraising), or the second choice (mostly supported by fees for some type of services provided or membership dues).

- If you are a church, select choice 3 and complete Schedule A (covered in Chapter 24).
- If you are a school, select choice 4, and complete Schedule B (covered in Chapter 25).
- If you are a hospital or medical research facility, select choice 5, and complete Schedule C (covered in Chapter 26).
- If you are an organization operated for the benefit of a college or university that is owned or operated by a governmental unit, select choice 6.
- If you are an agricultural research organization directly engaged in the continuous active conduct of agricultural research in conjunction with a college or university, select choice 7.
- If you are an organization supporting one or more 501(c) organizations, select choice 8, and complete Schedule D (covered in Chapter 27). You do not have to be supporting a 501(c) (3) organization (for example, you can support a 501(c) (4)).
- If you are doing testing for public safety, select choice 9.
- If you are a public charity and want IRS to decide your category, select choice 10.

- If you are going to be a foundation, select choice 11. This is not the right choice for most nonprofits.

Back to Foundation Classification:

Line 1. Select the foundation classification you are requesting from the list below.

- *You are described in 509(a)(1) and 170(b)(1)(A)(vi) as an organization that receives a substantial part of its financial support in the form of contributions from publicly supported organizations, from a governmental unit, or from the general public.*
- *You are described in 509(a)(2) as an organization that normally receives not more than one-third of its financial support from gross investment income and receives more than one-third of its financial support from contributions, membership fees, and*
- *gross receipts from activities related to its exempt functions (subject to certain exceptions).*
- *You are described in 509(a)(1) and 170(b)(1)(A)(i) as a church or a convention or association of churches. Complete Schedule A.*
- *You are described in 509(a)(1) and 170(b)(1)(A)(ii) as a school. Complete Schedule B.*
- *You are described in 509(a)(1) and 170(b)(1)(A)(iii) as a hospital, a cooperative hospital service organization, or a medical research organization operated in conjunction with a hospital. Complete Schedule C.*
- *You are described in 509(a)(1) and 170(b)(1)(A)(iv) as an organization operated for the benefit of a college or university that is owned or operated by a governmental unit.*
- *You are described in 509(a)(1) and 170(b)(1)(A)(ix) as an agricultural research organization directly engaged in*

the continuous active conduct of agricultural research in conjunction with a college or university.
- *You are described in 509(a)(3) as an organization supporting either one or more organizations described in 509(a)(1) or 509(a)(2) or a publicly supported section 501(c)(4), (5), or (6) organization. Complete Schedule D.*
- *You are described in 509(a)(4) as an organization organized and operated exclusively for testing for public safety.*
- *You are a publicly supported organization and would like the IRS to decide your correct classification.*
- *You are a private foundation.*

Line 1a. For Private Foundations Only (Otherwise, go to Line 2): As a private foundation, section 508(e) requires special provisions in your organizing document in addition to those that apply to all organizations described in section 501(c)(3). Check this box to confirm that your organizing document includes these provisions or you rely on state law.

A private foundation is one in which most of the support comes from predetermined sources such as a specific company or family. Private foundations pay some taxes on their investment income and cannot do as they want or invest where they want to. There are some restrictions that affect foundation operation, and with only a few exceptions, foundations must give away a percentage of their assets each year (minimum 5%). Not so with public charities. Also, public charities are allowed to work directly with individuals; foundations must work through other 501(c)(3) organizations to accomplish their missions unless they are private operating foundations.

The provisions (from IRS *Publication 557, Chapter 3, Section 501(c)(3) Organizations, Private Foundations*) that should be in your organizing documents for a foundation in addition to the ones required of all tax-exempt nonprofits include:

1. The corporation will distribute its income for each tax year at a time and in a manner as not to become subject to the tax on undistributed income imposed by section 4942 of the Internal Revenue Code, or the corresponding section of any future federal tax code.
2. The corporation won't engage in any act of self-dealing as defined in section 4941(d) of the Internal Revenue Code, or the corresponding section of any future federal tax code.
3. The corporation won't retain any excess business holdings as defined in section 4943(c) of the Internal Revenue Code, or the corresponding section of any future federal tax code.
4. The corporation won't make any investments in a manner as to subject it to tax under section 4944 of the Internal Revenue Code, or the corresponding section of any future federal tax code.
5. The corporation won't make any taxable expenditures as defined in section 4945(d) of the Internal Revenue Code, or the corresponding section of any future federal tax code.

Well over half the states require the mandatory provisions be included in the foundation's governing instruments. Details can be found in Revenue Ruling 75-038 located at *http://www.irs.gov/pub/irs-tege/rr75-038.pdf*. A list of states that allow you to rely on state law for the above foundation clauses are listed in Appendix B of this book. There are some exceptions as noted in Appendix B.

State specifically where your organizing document meets this requirement, such as a reference to a particular article or section in your organizing document (Page/Article/Paragraph) or state that you rely on state law.

Go to your incorporation document and find the page, article number, and paragraph for the required foundation clauses, or state that you "rely on state law." Check Appendix B to verify that you can rely on state law.

Line 1b. Do you or will you provide scholarships, fellowships, educational loans, or other educational grants to individuals, including grants for travel, study, or other similar purposes? If "Yes," complete Schedule H - Section II.

Answer "Yes" if you will be giving scholarships, fellowships, etc. and answer the questions for Schedule H. Instructions for Schedule H are in Chapter 31.

Line 1c. Are you a private operating foundation? To be a private operating foundation you must engage directly in the active conduct of charitable, religious, educational, and similar activities, as opposed to indirectly carrying out these activities by providing grants to individuals or other organizations.

If you answer "Yes," you have to answer Line 1d as well.

Line 1d. Describe how you meet the requirements for private operating foundation status, including how you meet the income test and either the assets test, the endowment test, or the support test. If you've been in existence for less than one year, describe how you are likely to satisfy the requirements for private operating foundation status.

IRS guidelines give specifics for private operating foundations:

> A private operating foundation is any private foundation that spends at least 85 percent of its adjusted net income or its minimum investment return, whichever is less, directly for the active conduct **of its exempt activities** (the income test).
>
> In addition, the foundation must meet one of the following tests:

The Assets Test

A private foundation will meet the assets test if 65% or more of its assets:

1. Are devoted directly to the active conduct of its exempt activity, a functionally related business, or a combination of the two,
2. Consist of stock of a corporation that is controlled by the foundation (by ownership of at least 80% of the total voting power of all classes of stock entitled to vote and at least 80% of the total shares of all other classes of stock) and at least 85% of the assets of which are so devoted, or
3. Are any combination of (1) and (2).

(More information at https://www.irs.gov/charities-non-profits/private-foundations/private-operating-foundation-assets-test)

The Endowment Test

A foundation will meet the endowment test if it normally makes qualifying distributions directly for the active conduct of its exempt activities of at least two-thirds of its *minimum investment return*.

(More information at https://www.irs.gov/charities-non-profits/private-foundations/private-operating-foundation-endowment-test)

The Support Test

A private foundation will meet the support test if:

1. At least 85 percent of its support (other than gross investment income) is normally received from the general public and 5 or more unrelated exempt organizations,
2. Not more than 25 percent of its support (other than gross investment income) is normally received from any one exempt organization, and
3. Not more than 50 percent of its support is normally received from gross investment income.

Here the term support means gifts, grants, contributions, membership fees, the value of services or facilities furnished by a governmental unit without charge, net income from unrelated business activities, and gross receipts from admissions, sales of merchandise, performance of services, or providing facilities in any activity that if not an unrelated trade or business.

The support received from any one exempt organization may be counted toward satisfying the 85 percent support test only if the foundation receives support from at least five exempt organizations.

(More information at *https://www.irs.gov/charities-non-profits/ private-foundations/private-operating-foundation-support-test*

Line 2. (This question does not apply if your organization has been in existence less than five years – go to next chapter).

If you have been in existence more than 5 years, you must confirm your public support status. To confirm your qualification as a public charity described in 509(a)(1) and 170(b)(1)(A)(vi) in existence for five or more tax years, you must have received one-

third or more of your total support from governmental agencies, contributions from the general public, and contributions or grants from other public charities; or 10% or more of your total support from governmental agencies, contributions from the general public, and contributions or grants from other public charities and the facts and circumstances indicate you are a publicly supported organization. Calculate whether you meet this support test for your most recent five-year period.

1. Did you receive contributions from any person, company, or organization whose gifts totaled more than the 2% amount of line 8 in Part VI-A?

    If "Yes," identify each person, company, or organization by letter (A, B, C, etc.) and indicate the amount contributed by each. Keep a list showing the name of and amount contributed by each of these donors for your records.

    To answer this question, if you received more than 2% of your revenues from one person or organization, you need to list the amounts in the box for question 2i. Instead of giving the names, assign each name a letter and list the amount given by each person or organization. For example:

    If John Smith donated $10,000, Sally Jones donated $15,000, and Henry Ward donated $6,000, and each of these donations were more than 2% of the revenue on Line 8 of the Financial Data page, you would type in:

    a. $10,000.
    b. $15,000.
    c. $ 6,000.

II. Based on your calculations, did you receive at least one-third of your support from public sources or did you normally receive at least 10 percent of your support from public sources and you have other characteristics of a publicly supported organization?

The answer must be "Yes" to qualify for public charity status. You figure it out by doing Form 990 Schedule A, Part II if you operate mostly on donations, and Part III if you operate on program service fee or membership fees.

CHAPTER 22

PARTS VIII, IX, AND X

EFFECTIVE DATE, ANNUAL FILING REQUIREMENTS, AND SIGNATURE

"Set your goals high, and don't stop till you get there."

—Bo Jackson

PART VIII. EFFECTIVE DATE.

In general, a determination letter recognizing exemption of an organization described in section 501(c)(3) is effective as of the date of formation of an organization if: (1) its purposes and activities prior to the date of the determination letter have been consistent with the requirements for exemption; and (2) it has filed an application for recognition of exemption within 27 months from the end of the month in which it was organized.

Line 1. Are you submitting this application within 27 months of the end of the month in which you were legally formed?

If you are a new organization, you are filing within 27 months of incorporating in your state. Mark "Yes" and go to the annual filing requirements section.

If you are just getting around to filing for 501(c) (3) tax-exempt status but more than 27 months have expired, you must do Schedule E. Mark "No," then click on Schedule E (covered in Chapter 28).

PART IX. ANNUAL FILING REQUIREMENTS

If you fail to file a required information return or notice for three consecutive years, your exempt status will be automatically revoked.

> **WARNING:** If you have been around for at least three years and have not filed your Form 990-series tax returns, DO NOT file this online application. IRS computers will calculate your incorporation date and realize you have not filed tax returns, and they will revoke your organization right after the approval is entered in the IRS computer. Instead, file all missing tax returns and *then* file the 501(c) (3) application. Make sure IRS has processed the returns before filing for 501(c) (3) tax-exempt status.

Line 1. Certain organizations are not required to file annual information returns or notices (Form 990, Form 990-EZ, or Form 990-N e-Postcard). If you are granted tax-exemption, are you claiming to be excused from filing Form 990, Form 990-EZ, or Form 990-N?

Unless you are a church or church organization or association of churches, mark "No" and go on to the signature page.

If you are a church, church organization, association of churches, or other similar organization, you will need to file Schedule A (instructions found in Chapter 24). You must make selections from the following:

If "Yes," are you claiming you are excepted from filing because you are:

- ✓ A church or association of churches
- ✓ An integrated auxiliary (such as a men's or women's organization, religious school, mission society, or religious group)
- ✓ A church-affiliated organization (other than a section 509(a)(3) organization) that is exclusively engaged in managing funds or maintaining retirement programs and is described in Revenue Procedure 96-10, 1996-1 C.B. 577
- ✓ A school below college level affiliated with a church or operated by a religious order
- ✓ A mission society (other than a section 509(a)(3) supporting organization) sponsored by, or affiliated with, one or more churches or church denominations, if more than half of the society's activities are conducted in, or directed at, persons in foreign countries
- ✓ An affiliate of a governmental unit that meets the requirements of Revenue Procedure 95-48, 1995-2 C.B. 418 (other than a section 509(a)(3) supporting organization)
- ✓ Other (describe)

I can tell you from personal experience that if you are not a church or an association of churches, or are not operating a religious school, the follow-up paperwork for any other 501(c)(3) listed in this area is unfathomable. IRS will send question after question and the process will continue until you tell them you withdraw your request to be exempt from filing annual information tax returns. I suggest you mark "No" if you are not a church or association of churches. You will save months and lots of headaches. If you are a church school, you will have to complete Schedule B (instructions in Chapter 25).

PART X. SIGNATURE

✓ **I declare under the penalties of perjury that I am authorized to sign this application on behalf of the above organization and that I have examined this application, and to the best of my knowledge it is true, correct, and complete.**

Add the name of the officer signing the application, their title and the date. When you (meaning an officer, director, or trustee) sign the application, you are certifying that everything you are submitting is true, correct, and complete to the best of your knowledge.

CHAPTER 23

UPLOAD CHECKLIST

"Money is only a tool. It will take you wherever you wish, but it will not replace you as the driver."

— AYN RAND

UPLOAD CHECKLIST:

- ✓ **Organizing document (and any amendments)**
- ✓ **Bylaws, if adopted**
- ✓ **Form 2848, Power of Attorney and Declaration of Representative (if applicable)**
- ✓ **Form 8821, Tax Information Authorization (if applicable)**
- ✓ **Supplemental responses (if applicable)**
- ✓ **Expedited handling request (if applicable)**

Check any boxes that apply, but you must include your incorporation and any amendments filed with the state, and your bylaws (make sure they have a date on them of when they were adopted).

If you have supplemental explanations for any of the questions, make sure to identify the Part and the Line (question) you are answering (for example: Part VI-A, Statement of Revenues and Expenses, Line 23).

If you have an attorney or tax professional handling your application, you can sign Form 2848, Power of Attorney and Declaration of Representative so IRS can talk with them about it.

If you have an individual who you would like to handle any IRS correspondence or communication, but they are not an attorney or CPA, you can upload Form 8821 Tax Information Authorization to give IRS permission to talk to and correspond with them instead of you.

EXPEDITED HANDLING REQUEST

If you have a donation or grant pending that you will lose if you do not get 501(c) (3) quickly, or if you are providing disaster relief or humanitarian aid and need approval *yesterday,* you have the option to request expedited handling at IRS. To do so, you must check the box for expedited handling and attach a letter explaining your need for immediate processing. A donation or grant of at least $5,000 from a disinterested person (not a board member or family) or organization will suffice. You must give IRS the name of the donor or grant maker, the amount of funding involved, and the date at which the funds will no longer be available if the 501(c) (3) is not approved. For humanitarian aid or disaster relief, tell IRS the current project you are working and why you need the 501(c) (3) status sooner than later.

ATTACHING YOUR DOCUMENTS TO THE APPLICATION

Make sure your organization name and EIN are at the top of every page you upload to your application. You will have to **combine your documents into one PDF document smaller than 15 MB**. If you are submitting just text, you will have no problem staying under 15 MB. Graphics and pictures are much larger files. If your files are larger than 15 MB, you need to call IRS at 877-829-5500 and ask them how to best submit the rest of the documents that will not fit the size limit. Just so you know, anything that is missing will be requested by letter from IRS, so even if you cannot upload it now, they will ask for it later if it is a required item such as incorporation document or bylaws. The trouble is that they wait several months before requesting the missing documents, so your application will be processed slowly if you do not attach everything they require.

WHAT IF I DON'T KNOW HOW TO COMBINE DOCUMENTS INTO ONE PDF?

Print all your documents or save them onto a thumb drive. Go to Staples or a print shop or office supply store and ask them to combine all your documents into one PDF and either put it on the thumb drive or email it to you.

PART III
IRS SCHEDULES FOR TAX-EXEMPT STATUS

CHAPTER 24

SCHEDULE A

CHURCHES

*"You must be the change you want
to see in the world."*

—Mahatma Gandhi

If it looks like a church, acts like a church, and functions like a church, it is probably a church. This classification includes mosques, temples, synagogues, etc. There must be a congregation or other membership. The church must have a denomination. Nondenominational churches may be granted religious organization 501(c) (3) status, but not church status.

IRS has some specific attributes it looks for to determine if you are a church according to their definition. You do not need to have all these attributes, but if some are missing that are typical for a church, or if the congregation is very small, it may create some thought of fraud or misrepresentation in the IRS agent's mind. Below is the list of attributes according to IRS. You do not have to have all fourteen to qualify for church status. However, some are more important than others. The items with asterisks are normally expected for approval as a church. If you do not have these yet (such as a large enough membership), just wait until you can meet the requirements to file. Churches are automatically tax-exempt under Section 501(c) (3) of the Internal Revenue Code, so you never have to file. Many churches choose to file to assure their tithing members that their contributions are tax deductible. If you choose to file, wait until you are big enough to cover the necessary items below:

- *A distinct legal existence* (Are you incorporated with the state as a church?)
- *A recognized creed and form of worship* (Do you have a denomination? A statement of faith? A written creed? What does a worship service look like in terms of how you conduct it? Do you sing hymns? Give testimonies? Present sermons? Have altar calls? Exactly what is your form of worship?)
- *A definite and distinct ecclesiastical government* (Do you have a pastor or equivalent? Do you have a system of who is in charge, a board, trustees, etc.?)
- *A formal code of doctrine and discipline* (What is your doctrine and what do you do when someone violates tenets of that doctrine?)
- *A distinct religious history* (History of your church and your denomination)
- *A membership not associated with any other church or denomination* (With few exceptions, IRS expects that members [not just attendees] of your church belong only to your church or denomination)
- *Ordained ministers ministering to the congregation* (qualified religious leaders with qualifications depending on the norms of the denomination)
- *Ordained ministers selected after completing prescribed courses of study* (What training does your religious leader have? How did he or she become ordained, licensed, or otherwise qualified to be a church leader, pastor, bishop, etc.?)
- *A literature of its own* (The Bible or other religious literature qualifies)
- *Established place of worship* (Do you have a stable location to meet? It can be rented, leased, owned, or borrowed).
- *Regular congregations* (IRS looks for a minimum of 20 - 25 congregation members who have met membership

requirements and have formally been accepted as members of the congregation. Not everyone who attends is a member. IRS wants a stable membership large enough to maintain a church. The congregation cannot be mostly one or two families; it must be from a number of families).
- *Regular religious services* (Do you have a schedule of service days and times that you follow?)
- *Sunday schools for the religious instruction of the young* (Do you provide religious training for children and youth?)
- *Schools for the preparation of ministers* (Do you have some type of discipleship program to grow new church leaders?)

Line 1. Do you have a written creed, statement of faith, or summary of beliefs? If "Yes," describe your written creed, statement of faith, or summary of beliefs.

Your denomination, written creed, statement of faith, or summary of beliefs must be included. If it is larger than the box for Line 1 allows, write "See Attached" and add it to the uploaded documents before submission of the application.

Line 2. Do you have a literature of your own? If "Yes," describe your literature.

This includes any writings containing practices, rules, laws, doctrines, history, as well as your religious book you teach from such as the Bible.

Line 3. Do you have a formal code of doctrine and discipline? If "Yes," describe your code of doctrine and discipline.

These are the laws, rules, and requirements of your denomination, or the tenets of your faith. Also explain how your church handles someone who breaks those rules, laws, requirements, or tenets of faith.

Line 4. Describe your religious hierarchy or ecclesiastical government.

Who is in charge of your church? How are they put into that role? Is there a church board? How are they placed on the board? Do you have trustees? Who appoints or elects them? What is the chain of command in the church (and denomination if that plays a role in your ecclesiastical government)?

Line 5. Are you part of a group of churches with similar beliefs and structures? If "Yes," explain.

If you are part of a convention, association, or union of churches, include the name of the group you are part of. Most churches applying for 501(c)(3) status will answer "No." This question is not asking you if you are a Southern Baptist, or part of the Catholic church. It is asking if you fall under a parent organization's 501(c)(3) umbrella. If you are applying for your own 501(c)(3), then you will not be part of a group exemption, you will have your own exemption.

If you are leaving a group exemption, then explain why you are leaving. We had one client who was a pastor of a Holiness church. The parent organization's doctrine stated that men could not wear neckties. Several members of this church's congregation were bankers, attorneys, and other professionals who had to wear a tie to work. The church filed for their own 501(c)(3) tax-exempt status and removed the restriction on neckties in their church constitution. That was their explanation for leaving the group exemption and getting their own exemption outside the umbrella of the parent organization. If you are under another church's group exemption or umbrella, you can get your own exemption without any reason except

> **The parent organization's doctrine stated that men could not wear neckties.**

that you want to be independent of the parent organization, or that you are finally big enough to function as an independent church and choose to do so.

Line 6. Do you have a form of worship? If "Yes," describe your form of worship.

What are the practices of your church that show your dedication to your beliefs?

Line 7. Do you have regularly scheduled religious services? If "Yes," describe the nature of the services.

Give days of the week and times of your services for the different ministries you conduct. Explain how a normal religious gathering proceeds. Many churches start with Worship, then a message from the religious leader, then prayer, then offering, etc. IRS just wants to know what happens at your services.

Line 7a. What is the average attendance at your regularly scheduled religious services?

IRS likes to see at least 20 - 25 people attending your religious services. Very small numbers in attendance are suspect to IRS, especially if most of the members are from one or two families.

Line 8. Do you have an established place of worship? If "Yes," describe your established place of worship or where you meet to hold regularly scheduled religious services.

You do not need to own the location used to conduct services. You can rent it, or it can be provided to you at no charge. If you do not have a location, where are you meeting? Not having a location can cause IRS to downgrade you to a religious organization instead of giving you church status.

Line 9. Do you have an established congregation or other regular membership group? If "No," continue to Line 10.

If you want church status, the answer is "Yes," although we did get a House of Prayer approved in Arizona that had no congregation. It was there to give a place of prayer for religious leaders and the community to come and pray anytime they wanted without attending a scheduled service.

Line 9a. How many members do you have?

IRS likes to see at least 20 members.

Line 9b. Do you have a process by which an individual becomes a member? If "Yes," describe the process.

Answer "Yes" if you keep records of who is currently a member. If all your members are from the same family, you are not classified as a church. Give IRS the details requested to determine how a person would become a member of your church and what the benefits of that membership would be. Attach a copy of an application if one exists. Don't create a membership application if you don't have one, IRS will approve you without one. Make sure your membership requirements answer given here matches what is in your bylaws or church constitution.

Line 9c. Do your members have voting rights, rights to participate in religious functions, or other rights? If "Yes," describe the rights your members have.

Voting rights might be given at annual member meetings to elect new trustees, special meetings to vote on purchases of land, to approve the annual budget, etc. Members would be allowed to participate in church activities, religious services, community ministries, etc.

Line 9d. May your members be associated with another denomination or church?

The answer is normally "No." However, there are a few denominations that allow it.

Line 9e. Are all of your members part of the same family?

Don't apply if all your members are part of the same family. IRS will not give you church status.

Line 10. Do you conduct baptisms, weddings, funerals, or other religious rites?

Most churches do some or all of these.

Line 11. Do you have a school for the religious instruction of the young?

This is referring to Sunday School or similar programs for children.

Line 12. Do you have ministers or religious leaders? If "Yes," describe these roles and explain whether the ministers or religious leaders are ordained, commissioned, or licensed after a prescribed course of study.

What training has your minister or religious leader completed? Self-ordination, self-study, or methods that did not include a formal course of instruction and learning do not qualify as a prescribed course of study. Some denominations have ordination boards. If yours is one, explain the process for your denomination.

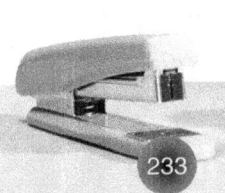

Line 13. Do you have schools for the preparation of your ordained ministers or religious leaders?

This is not required to get church status, but mark "Yes" if you prepare religious leaders through a curriculum or classes to serve in the church or denomination.

Line 14. Do you ordain, commission, or license ministers or religious leaders? If "Yes," describe the requirements for ordination, commission, or licensure.

This is not a requirement for church status, and you can answer "No." However, if you plan to ordain, commission, or license ministers or religious leaders in the future, best to answer this question now so you are approved ahead of time.

Line 15. Do you have other information you believe should be considered regarding your status as a church? If "Yes," explain.

Is there anything else you want IRS to know to decide if you qualify for tax exemption as a church? We suggest you answer this question like this (feel free to copy!):

> *We do not attempt to influence legislation or intervene in any way in political campaigns other than to vote our conscience on election days.*

> *We are not already exempt under a group-ruling letter of a parent organization, and are not part of a conference, convention, or association of churches.*

> *Under IRC § 508(c), churches are not required to apply for recognition of exemption with IRS to be treated as an organization described in IRC § 501(c) (3). We already meet the requirements without applying, but choose to seek formal recognition of exemption.*

CHAPTER 25

SCHEDULE B

SCHOOLS, COLLEGES, AND UNIVERSITIES

"He who opens a school door closes a prison."
—Victor Hugo

Not all schools are created equal, and not all educational organizations qualify for tax-exempt school status. You can be approved as a regular 501(c)(3) though if you have a charitable mission. Your organization is only qualified for school status if your main activity is conducting formal instruction, if you have scheduled habitual customary curriculum, qualified teachers, an identifiable student body taking classes on a regular basis, and there is an identifiable location for these classes and students to meet to conduct this formal, habitual, scheduled curricular instruction. Sounds like a mouthful, but it is IRS making sure you actually are conducting instruction, not running a diploma mill.

IRS' definition of *school* includes "primary, secondary, preparatory, high schools, colleges, and universities." IRS has started approving virtual schools for K-12 education.

Homeschools do not qualify for tax-exempt status but homeschool associations do qualify if they are formed to provide educational activities for students who are homeschooled.

Line 1. Do you normally have a regularly scheduled curriculum, a regular faculty of qualified teachers, a regularly enrolled student body, and facilities where your educational activities are regularly carried on?

Answer "Yes" or "No" depending on the details of your organization.

Line 2. Is the primary function of your school the presentation of formal instruction? If "No," continue to Line 3.

If you answered "Yes," then answer 2a. Otherwise, go on to Line 3. If you answered "No," you might want to rethink your classification choice as a school and go back to Part VIII, Line 1 and select a different choice besides school.

Line 2a. Select the best description(s) of your school:

- ✓ **Elementary school**
- ✓ **Secondary school**
- ✓ **Charter school**
- ✓ **College or university**
- ✓ **Technical school**
- ✓ **Other school (describe)**

If you are a K-12 school, you can select elementary and secondary. Select all that apply. For "Other school," describe the type of school you will have that does not fall into one of the other categories.

Line 3. Are you a public school because you are operated by a state or subdivision of a state or operated wholly or predominantly from government funds or property? If "Yes," explain how you are operated by a state or subdivision of a state. Do not complete the remainder of Schedule B.

You might explain that you have a contract with and are receiving funds from local or state government. Enter any other details that explain your situation. If you answered "Yes," you can stop Schedule B here and go on to the rest of the application for 501(c) (3).

Line 4. Were you formed or substantially expanded at the time of public school desegregation in the school district or county in which you are located?

Desegregation took place decades ago, so more than likely, your answer is "No."

These next questions seek to determine if you discriminate based on race, color, and national or ethnic origin. If you do, you do not qualify for tax-exempt status. Include a copy of your bylaws containing your nondiscrimination policy. If it is not included in your formal organizing or operating documents, include a copy of your signed resolution approving a nondiscrimination policy.

Line 5. Has a state or federal administrative agency or judicial body ever determined that you are racially discriminatory? If "Yes," explain.

If you are a new entity, the answer is "No." Hopefully, the answer is "No" anyway. If not, explain the details in the box provided.

Line 6. Has your right to receive financial aid or assistance from a governmental agency ever been revoked or suspended? If "Yes," explain.

If you are a brand new entity, the answer is "No." Hopefully, the answer is "No" anyway. If not, explain the details in the box provided.

Information Required by Revenue Procedure 75-50 as Modified by Revenue Procedure 2019-22

Line 7. Have you adopted a racially nondiscriminatory policy as to students in your organizing document, bylaws, or by resolution of your governing body?

If you do not, you must approve a resolution implementing one, or add the wording to your bylaws. If not, you will be denied tax-exempt status.

Revenue Procedure 75-50 located at *http://www.irs.gov/pub/irs-tege/rp1975-50.pdf* requires that you not only have a racially nondiscrimination policy but that you also publicize it. However, in 2019, IRS updated their guidelines in Revenue Procedure 2019-22 located at *https://www.irs.gov/pub/irs-drop/rp-19-22.pdf* to include putting your nondiscriminatory policy on your website instead of having to publish it annually in a newspaper of general circulation. The policy must be prominent on the website and be there year-round, and a visitor to the primary landing page must be able to see it without signing in.

Here is the new wording, which has changed only slightly from the previous wording:

NOTICE OF NONDISCRIMINATORY POLICY AS TO STUDENTS

The _____ School admits students of any race, color, national and ethnic origin to all the rights, privileges, programs, and activities generally accorded or made available to students at the school. It does not discriminate on the basis of race, color, national and ethnic origin in administration of its educational policies, admissions policies, scholarship and loan programs, and athletic and other school-administered programs.

Line 8. Do your brochures, application forms, advertisements, and catalogues dealing with student admissions, programs, and scholarships contain a statement of your racially nondiscriminatory policy? If "Yes," continue to Line 9.

Nondiscrimination statements must be included in all brochures, advertisements, catalogs, and other printed materials given to the public and the student body. You can include the entire Nondiscriminatory Policy or you can use these words on printed materials:

> "The _____ School admits students of any race, color, and national or ethnic origin."

If you answered no, you must check 8a.

Line 8a. By checking this box, you agree that all future printed materials, including website content, will contain the required nondiscriminatory policy statement.

Check the box if you do not answer "Yes" to question 8.

Line 9. Have you made your racially nondiscriminatory policy known to all segments of the general community you serve by: a) publishing a notice of your policy in a newspaper of general circulation that serves all racial segments of the community; b) publicizing your policy over broadcast media in a way that is reasonably expected to be effective; or c) displaying a notice of your policy at all times on your primary, publicly accessible internet home page in a manner reasonably expected to be noticed by visitors to the homepage? If "Yes," continue to Line 10.

If you answer "No," check box 9a.

Line 9a. By checking this box, you agree that you will publicize your nondiscriminatory policy in a way that meets the requirements of Revenue Procedure 75-50, 1975-2 C.B. 587, as modified by Revenue Procedure 2019-22, I.R.B. 1260.

If you answered "No" to Line 9, check line 9a.

Line 10. Do or will you (or any department or division of your organization) discriminate in any way on the basis of race with respect to admissions, use of facilities or exercise of student privileges, faculty or administrative staff, or scholarship or loan programs? If "Yes," for any of the above, explain fully.

The answer is "No."

If you answer "Yes" for any reason, explain your answer, but expect to be turned down for 501(c)(3) tax-exempt status.

Line 11. Complete the table below to show the racial composition for the current academic year and projected for the next academic year. If you are not operational, submit an estimate based on the best information available (such as the racial composition of the community you serve). For each racial category, enter the number of (a) students, (b) faculty, and (c) administrative staff. Provide actual numbers rather than percentages for each racial category.

Here is where you give numbers (not percentages) of students, faculty, and staff and administrators based on racial composition. Depending on where you are and the racial composition of your community, you might include numbers for Caucasian, Black, Hispanic, and Asia-Pacific students. IRS wants to know about the current year and next year. If your school will not be open until after next year, put in all zeros. Otherwise, give it your best guess.

Here is an example of a small private school that will not be open until next year:

Racial Category	(a) Student Body		(b) Faculty		(c) Administrative Staff	
	Current Year	Next Year	Current Year	Next Year	Current Year	Next Year
Caucasian	0	25	0	2	0	1
Black	0	32	0	3	0	2
Hispanic	0	17	0	1	0	0
Asia-Pacific	0	3	0	0	0	0
Total	0	77	0	6	0	3

Line 12. In the table below, enter the number and amount of loans and scholarships awarded to enrolled students by racial categories. Provide actual numbers rather than percentages for each racial category.

If you do not provide loans and scholarships, check the box that says:

WISCONSIN

Check here if you will not provide any loans or scholarships to students.

From the example above, here are how the numbers might look for a school that is not opening until next year and provides partial scholarships to students with financial need in the amount of $2,500 per school year. If you do not know the exact numbers, give it your best guess based on the racial composition of the community you will serve.

If you give loans or scholarships, be sure to also fill out Schedule H.

Racial Category	Number of Loans		Number of Loans		Number of Scholarships		Amount of Scholarships	
	Current Year	Next Year	Current Year	Next Year	Current Year	Next Year	Current Year	Next Year
Caucasian	0	0	0	0	0	10	0	25,000
Black	0	0	0	0	0	15	0	37,500
Hispanic	0	0	0	0	0	5	0	7,500
Asia-Pacific	0	0	0	0	0	0	0	0
Total	0	0	0	0	0	0	0	75,000

Line 13. List your incorporators, founders, board members, and donors of land or buildings, whether individuals or organizations.

In the box, list the incorporator(s), founders, board members, and donors of land or buildings, and specify which role they are in.

Line 14. Do any of your incorporators, founders, board members, and donors of land or buildings, whether individuals or organizations, have an objective to maintain segregated public or private school education? If "Yes," explain.

The correct answer is "No." If you answer "Yes," give an explanation of why and don't expect to get approved for 501(c)(3) status.

Line 15. Will you maintain records according to the nondiscrimination provisions contained in Revenue Procedure 75-50? If "No," explain.

The answer is "Yes." What does it mean? It means that if you must file annual Form 990-series tax returns, you will keep records to give the racial composition of students, faculty, and staff and administrators on those returns. If you are not required to file a tax return, you will keep records of racial composition and instead of a tax return, you will submit IRS Form 5578, Annual Certification of Racial Nondiscrimination for Private Schools no later than the 15th day of the fifth month after the fiscal year end. You must maintain records for at least three years.

CHAPTER 26

SCHEDULE C

HOSPITALS AND MEDICAL RESEARCH ORGANIZATIONS

> *"Healing is a matter of time, but it is sometimes also a matter of opportunity."*
>
> —Hippocrates

If you are a cooperative hospital service organization, you do not need to fill out Schedule C. It is only used if you are a hospital or medical research organization operated in combination with a hospital. If the main function of an organization is medical treatment services, it qualifies as a medical care facility even though it may be operating on an outpatient basis. Treatment can be for physical or mental conditions and includes drug treatment centers.

The definition of *hospital* does not include convalescent homes, children's or elderly homes, or institutions providing job training for the handicapped.

According to IRS guidelines, a medical research organization is one whose *"principal purpose or function is the direct, continuous, and active conduct of medical research in conjunction with a hospital."* In addition, IRS requires that *"the research must be to discover, develop, or verify knowledge relating to the causes, diagnosis, treatment, prevention, or control of human physical or mental diseases and impairments."*

Medical Research Organizations

Line 1. Are you a medical research organization (an organization whose principal purpose or function is medical research and which is directly engaged in the continuous active conduct of medical research) operated in conjunction with a hospital? If "No," continue to Line 2.

If you answered "Yes," you must answer the following questions:

Line 1a. Name the hospitals with which you have a relationship and describe the relationship.

Provide a list of all hospitals you work with, describe the nature of the interaction and relationships, and it is a good idea to attach copies of all agreements.

Line 1b. List your assets showing their fair market value and the portion of your assets directly devoted to medical research.

List your assets, their fair market value, and what percentage of each asset is being used for research.

You do not have to answer any other questions in Schedule C.

Cooperative Hospital Service Organization

Line 1. Are you a medical research organization (an organization whose principal purpose or function is medical research and which is directly engaged in the continuous active conduct of medical research) operated in conjunction with a hospital? If "No," continue to Line 2.

Answer "No."

Line 2. Are you applying for exemption as a cooperative hospital service organization described in section 501(e)? If "Yes," explain.

According to IRS guidelines:

"A cooperative hospital service organization performs one or more of the specific services listed below for one or more exempt hospitals on a cooperative basis. The services listed below are exclusive. A cooperative service organization that provides services other than those listed below, or that provides services to an organization other than an exempt hospital, doesn't qualify for exemption under section 501(c)(3). The list of services includes:

1. *Data processing;*
2. *Purchasing (including the purchasing of insurance on a group basis);*
3. *Warehousing;*
4. *Billing and collection (including the purchasing of patron accounts receivable on a recourse basis);*
5. *Food;*
6. *Clinical;*
7. *Industrial engineering;*
8. *Laboratory;*
9. *Printing;*
10. *Communications;*
11. *Record center; and*
12. *Personnel services (including selection testing, training, and education of personnel).*

If you answered "Yes," do not complete the rest of Schedule C.

Hospitals

Line 1. Are you a medical research organization (an organization whose principal purpose or function is medical research and which is directly engaged in the continuous active conduct of medical research) operated in conjunction with a hospital? If "No," continue to Line 2.

Answer "No."

Line 2. Are you applying for exemption as a cooperative hospital service organization described in section 501(e)? If "Yes," explain.

Answer "No."

Line 3. Are all the doctors in the community eligible for staff privileges? If "No," give the reasons why and explain how the medical staff is selected.

If all doctors in your area have staff privileges or are only restricted due to capacity, then mark "Yes." If "No," describe how you determine which courtesy staff have privileges at your facility and the exact criteria and selection procedures used.

Line 4. Do or will you provide medical services to all individuals in your community who can pay for themselves or are able to pay through some form of insurance? If "No," explain.

Answer "Yes" if you accept all patients in the community who can pay or who have Medicare, Medicare, or insurance.

If you restrict admission in any of these categories, you must provide an in-depth explanation of how and why you restrict patient admittance to exclude any of these categories.

Line 5. Do you or will you maintain a full-time emergency room? If "Yes," continue to Line 6.

If you have 24/7 emergency room care, answer "Yes." If not, answer Line 5a.

Line 5a. Are you a specialty hospital or would emergency services be duplicative based on your region or locality?

Explain why you do not provide emergency services.

Line 6. Do you provide free or below cost services? If "Yes," describe your policy for determining when and to whom you provide these services and how these services promote the organization's benefit to the community.

If you answered "Yes," what provisions do you have to treat emergencies when someone cannot pay? Do you have a written policy? Do you have written or verbal agreements with first responders concerning emergency services? Describe them and include copies of written policies and agreements in the attachment at the end of the application. If you have verbal agreements, explain them in detail to include how and when the agreements were made.

Line 7. Do you or will you carry on a formal program of medical training or medical research? If "Yes," describe such programs, including the type of programs offered, the scope of such programs, and affiliations with other hospitals or medical care providers with which you carry on the medical training or research programs.

If "Yes," include details of how your program works and any organizational affiliations.

Line 8. Do you or will you carry on a formal program of community education? If "Yes," describe such programs, including the type of programs offered, the scope of such programs, and affiliation with other hospitals or medical care providers with which you offer community education programs.

If "Yes," include the details of the programs you have or plan to have, and how you will interact with the other hospitals or medical professionals to offer the programs.

Line 9. Is your board of directors composed of a majority of individuals who are representative of the community you serve, or do you operate under a parent organization whose board of directors is composed of a majority of individuals who are representative of the community you serve? If "Yes," continue to Line 10.

This question seeks to ascertain whether your board of directors is representative of the community where you are located. IRS instructions for this item give this guidance:

> *Answer "Yes" if you have a board of directors that is representative of the community you serve.*
>
> *Answer "Yes" if an organization described in section 501(c)(3) with a community board exercises rights or powers over you, such as the right to appoint members to your governing board of directors and the power to approve certain transactions.*
>
> *Answer "Yes" if you are subject to a state corporate practice of medicine law that requires your governing board to be composed solely of physicians licensed to practice medicine in the state.*

If you answer "No," then you must answer Line 9a.

Line 9a. List each board member's name and business, financial, or professional relationship with the hospital. Also, identify each board member who is representative of the community and describe how that individual is a community representative. If you operate under a parent organization whose board of directors is not composed of a majority of individuals who are representative of the community you serve, provide the requested information for your parent's board of directors as well.

You may not have enough room to provide all that information in the box provided, so you might want to include it in an attachment at the end of the application. In that case, type in "See Attachment."

Line 10. Do you operate a facility which is required by a state to be licensed, registered, or similarly recognized as a hospital? If "No," do not complete the rest of Schedule C.

If "No," you are done with this schedule.

If "Yes," you must complete the following:

Line 10a. Do you conduct a community health needs assessment (CHNA) at least once every three years and adopt an implementation strategy to meet the community health needs identified in the assessment as required by section 501(r)(3)? If "No," explain.

IRS guidelines state:

> *A community health needs assessment (CHNA) is an assessment of the significant health needs of the community. To meet the requirements of section 501(r)(3), a CHNA must take into account input from persons who represent the broad interests of the community served by the hospital*

facility, including those with special knowledge of or expertise in public health, and must be made widely available to the public. Each hospital facility must conduct a CHNA at least once every 3 years and adopt an implementation strategy to meet the community health need identified through such CHNA.

Answer "Yes," if the hospital facility conducted a complying CHNA in the current tax year or in either of the 2 immediately preceding tax years or if the hospital facility intends to conduct a CHNA before the end of its first 3-year period.

If "No," you may not get 501(c)(3) status because you will not meet the 501(r)(3) hospital requirements necessary to get 501(c)(3) tax-exempt status. These regulations work together for hospitals.

Line 10b. Do you have a written financial assistance policy (FAP) and a written policy relating to emergency medical care as required by section 501(r)(4)? If "No," explain.

Answer "Yes" if you have a written policy.

IRS guidelines specify:

A financial assistance policy (FAP), sometimes referred to as a charity care policy, is a policy describing how an organization will provide financial assistance at its hospital(s) and other facilities, if any. Financial assistance includes free or discounted health services provided to persons who meet the organization's criteria for financial assistance and are unable to pay for all or a portion of the services.

Line 10c. Do you both (1) limit amounts charged for emergency or other medically necessary care provided to individuals eligible for assistance under your FAP to not more than amounts generally billed to individuals who have insurance covering such care, and (2) prohibit use of gross charges as required by section 501(r)(5)? If "No," explain.

Section 501(r) (5) sets the most that can be charged to no more than you would bill for services when a patient has insurance coverage. You can answer "Yes" if you initially overcharged, but refunded the overpayment after the Financial Assistance application was approved. You can review the 501 (r) regulations for Affordable Care Act at *https://www.irs.gov/charities-non-profits/charitable-organizations/requirements-for-501c3-hospitals-under-the-affordable-care-act-section-501r*

Line 10d. Do you make reasonable efforts to determine whether an individual is FAP-eligible before engaging in extraordinary collection actions as required by section 501(r)(6)? If "No," explain.

The correct answer is "Yes."

CHAPTER 27

SCHEDULE D

SECTION 509(A) (3) SUPPORTING ORGANIZATIONS

LUCK: Laboring Under Correct Knowledge.
—PAUL CRUMP

You have to complete Schedule D because you said you are an organization that only gives money to other nonprofit organizations. This is common when you are a supporting arm of an established tax-exempt organization that doesn't want to detract from its nonprofit mission to raise funds. So, you are the fundraising body that supports the other organization. This is permissible as long as you maintain control, but several possibilities exist that you may be controlled (in the eyes of IRS) by "disqualified persons."

Electing this schedule has many technical applications, and we strongly suggest you seek the help of a tax professional before filing to eliminate months of follow-up paperwork to meet the intent and the letter of the law for IRS. The technicalities are beyond the scope of this book. It is a book in itself and is worth every cent you spend to get a professional to complete this schedule. You may want to go back and see if this is the best selection under Part VII (Foundation Classification). If another less complicated selection is possible, you may want to choose it. However, if you are still sure you want to file Schedule D, here are some basic guidance and resources to figure out the technicalities. If in doubt, contact IRS and talk to them about your specific circumstances before filing.

First of all, you can qualify as a public charity under Section 509(a) (3) if you operate entirely to benefit, perform the functions of, or carry out the purposes of one or more public charities listed in Section 509 (a) (1). This will include organizations that get their funding from a wide range of sources, such as churches, schools, hospitals, etc. You can also qualify as a public charity if you exclusively benefit Section 509(a) (2) organizations, which include organizations that get their funds from grants, donations, or fees for their nonprofit purpose.

You can also qualify as a supporting organization if you are supporting the charitable purposes of 501(c) (4) organizations (civic leagues, social welfare organizations, local associations of employees), 501(c) (5) organizations (labor, agriculture, and horticultural organizations), or 501(c) (6) organizations (business leagues, chambers of commerce, and real estate boards).

Line 1: List the names, addresses, and EINs of the organizations you support.

Write the names, addresses, and employer identification number (FEIN) of every organization you support. If they will not all fit in the box provided, write "See Attachment" and include the list in the attachment you upload at the end of the application.

Line 2: Are all your supported organizations public charities under section 509(a)(1) or (2)? If "Yes," continue to Line 3.

In a nutshell, both those sections include organizations with 501(c) (3) tax-exempt status, but 509(a) (1) organizations get their support from donations, grants, etc., and 509(a) (2) have some sort of revenue stream that is derived from either membership dues or charging for program services provided. In either case, they are both public charities. Foundations normally are neither 509(a) (1) or 509(a) (2) because they get their revenues from very limited sources such as family members for a family foundation, or from a corporation for a corporate foundation.

If you are supporting public charities, mark "Yes."

If you are not supporting public charities, mark "No," and answer Line 2a.

Line 2a. Are your supported organizations tax exempt under section 501(c)(4), 501(c)(5), or 501(c)(6) and do your supported organizations meet the public support test under section 509(a)(2)? If "No," explain how each organization you support is a public charity under section 509(a)(1) or 509(a)(2).

The organizations listed in this question include 501(c) (4) organizations such as civic leagues, social welfare organizations, local associations of employees; 501(c) (5) organizations such as labor, agriculture, and horticultural organizations; and 501(c) (6) organizations such as business leagues, chambers of commerce, and real estate boards.

The public support test for 509(a)(2) is that normally the organization receives not more than one-third of its financial support from gross investment income and receives more than one-third of its financial support from contributions, membership fees, and gross receipts from activities related to its exempt functions (subject to certain exceptions).

The easy answer is "Yes." If not, explain how the organizations you support meet the requirements of publicly supported tax-exempt organizations.

Line 3. Which of the following describes your relationship with your supported organization(s)?

- ✓ **A majority of your governing board or officers are elected or appointed by your supported organization(s). (Type I supporting organization)**
- ✓ **Your control or management is vested in the same persons who control or manage your supported organization(s). (Type II supporting organization)**
- ✓ **One or more of your officers, directors, or trustees are elected or appointed by the officers, directors, trustees, or membership of your supported organization(s), or one or more of your officers, directors, trustees, or other important office holders, are also members of the governing body of your supported organization(s), or your officers, directors, or trustees maintain a close and continuous working relationship with the officers, directors, or trustees of your supported organization(s). (Type III supporting organization)**

You must select one of the three choices to show under Section 501(a) (3) of the IRS Code that you meet the relationship test for the organization(s) you choose to support. Pick the one that best describes your relationship with your supported organization(s).

Line 4. Describe how your governing board and officers are selected. If you are a Type III organization, also describe how your officers, directors, or trustees maintain a close and continuous working relationship with the officers, directors, or trustees of your supported organization(s).

How do you select board members and board officers?

Line 5. Do any persons who are disqualified persons (except individuals who are disqualified persons only because they are foundation managers) with respect to you or persons who have a family or business relationship with any disqualified persons appoint any of your foundation managers? If "Yes," (1) describe the process by which disqualified persons appoint any of your foundation managers, (2) provide the names of these disqualified persons and the foundation managers they appoint, and (3) explain how control is vested over your operations (including assets and activities) by persons other than disqualified persons.

Organizations controlled directly or indirectly by disqualified people make the organization ineligible for public charity status. Section 4946 of the IRS code gives the following guidelines on who is a disqualified person:

- Substantial Contributor (normally more than $5,000 a year if that is more than 2% of the total contributions of the previous year)
- Foundation manager (includes officers, directors, and trustees)
- Owner of more than 20% interest in an organization that is a substantial contributor
- Family members. IRS defines family members to include an individual's spouse, ancestors, lineal descendants, and the spouses of his or her lineal descendants. Also, the legally adopted child of an individual is his or her child within the meaning of this regulation. Internal Revenue Code (IRC) 4946(d) provides that the family of any individual shall include only his spouse, ancestors, children, grandchildren, great grandchildren, and the spouses of children, grandchildren, and great grandchildren. Also includes the surviving spouse of a child, grandchild, or great grandchild of a substantial contributor (until remarriage).
- Persons who hold more than a 35% interest
- Government official

Hopefully, the answer is "No." If not, describe how disqualified persons appoint any of your foundation managers, give the names of these disqualified persons and the foundation managers they appoint, and explain how control is vested over your operations (including assets and activities) by persons other than disqualified persons.

Line 6. Do any persons who are disqualified persons (except individuals who are disqualified persons only because they are foundation managers) have any influence regarding your operations, including your assets or activities? If "Yes," (1) provide the names of these disqualified persons, (2) explain how influence is exerted over your operations (including assets and activities), and (3) explain how control is vested over your operations (including assets and activities) by individuals other than disqualified persons.

Hopefully, the answer is "No." If "Yes," give the name of the disqualified persons, tell how they influence your operations, activities, and/or assets, and explain how you are maintaining control over your operations.

Line 7. Does your organizing document specify your supported organization(s) by name? If "Yes" and you selected Type I above, continue to Line 8. If "Yes," and you selected Type II, do not complete the rest of Schedule D. If "No" and you selected Type III above, amend your organizing document to specify your supported organization(s) by name or you will not meet the organizational test and need to reconsider your requested public charity classification; then continue to Line 8.

If you exist to support specific organizations, they should be named in your organizing document (Articles of Incorporation by whatever name the state calls it).

If on Line 3, you selected Type 1 and you can answer "Yes" to this question, continue.

If on Line 3, you selected Type II, and you can answer "Yes" to this question, you can stop Schedule D now.

If on Line 3, you selected Type III, and you answer "No" to this question, you will have to file an amendment to your Articles of Incorporation, or you should go back to the question on Foundation Classification and choose a different charitable category. If you still want to be a supporting organization, continue to Line 8.

Line 8. Do you or will you receive contributions from any person who alone, or combined with family members or an entity at least 35% controlled by that person, controls any of your supported organizations, or will you receive contributions from any family member of, or an entity at least 35% controlled by, any person who controls any of your supported organizations? If "Yes," explain. If you selected Type I above, do not complete the rest of Schedule D.

For most organizations, the answer is "No." If "Yes," explain.

If you chose Type I on Line 3, you are done with Schedule D. Otherwise, continue.

Line 9. Do the officers, directors, or trustees of your supported organization have a significant voice in your investment policies, the timing and making of grants, the selection of grant recipients, and in otherwise directing the use of your income or assets? If "Yes," explain.

Line 9 question is a Type III responsiveness test. IRS says to:

Answer "Yes," if, because of your relationship described in Line 3, the supported organization has a significant involvement in your investment policies, making and timing of grants, and directing the use of your income and assets, and explain how your supported organization is involved in these matters.

Line 10. In each taxable year, do you or will you provide each of your supported organizations with (a) a written notice addressed to a principal officer of the supported organization describing the type and amount of all of the support you provided to the supported organization during the immediately preceding taxable year, (b) a copy of your most recently filed Form 990-series return or notice, and (c) a copy of your governing documents? If 'No,' explain.

The correct answer is "Yes." If not, explain why you will not do these things. This question is also on your annual tax-exempt information return (Form 990-series filing).

Type III Organizations

IRS guidance on Type III organizations includes:

An organization seeking classification as a Type III supporting organization must meet an integral part test, which is satisfied by maintaining significant involvement in the operations of one or more supported organizations and providing support on which the supported organization(s) are dependent. A Type III supporting organization may be functionally integrated (lines 11–12) or non-functionally integrated (lines 13 and 13a–c) depending on the manner in which it meets the integral part test. Functionally integrated Type III supporting organizations are subject to fewer restrictions and requirements than non-functionally integrated Type III supporting organizations.

Line 11. Do you exercise a substantial degree of direction over the policies, programs, and activities of your supported organization(s) and appoint or elect (directly or indirectly) a majority of the officers, directors, or trustees of your supported organization(s)? If "Yes," explain.

IRS Guidelines for this question are:

Answer "Yes," if you're the parent of all your supported organizations because you:

1. *Have the power to appoint or elect, directly or indirectly, a majority of the officers, directors, or trustees of each supported organization; and*
2. *Exercise a substantial degree of direction over the policies, programs, and activities of each supported organization.*

Line 12. Do substantially all of your activities directly further the exempt purposes of one or more supported organizations to which you are responsive by performing the functions of, or carrying out the purposes of, such supported organization(s) and but for your involvement would normally be engaged in by such supported organization(s). If "Yes," explain and do not complete the rest of Schedule D.

IRS guidelines on this question include:

Answer "Yes," if you conduct activities that the supported organization would otherwise need to conduct in furtherance of its exempt purposes and describe the activities that you conduct. Holding title to and managing assets that are used (or held for use) directly in carrying out the exempt purposes of your supported organization (exempt-use assets) are activities that directly further the exempt purposes of your supported organization. Conversely, with certain exceptions, fundraising, making grants (whether to the supported organization or to third parties), and investing and managing non-exempt-use assets aren't activities that directly further the exempt purposes of the supported organization. See Regulations section 1.509(a)-4(i)(4) (ii) for more information.

If you answer "Yes" to this question, explain how your activities directly further the exempt purposes of the supported organizations, and then you are finished with Schedule D.

Line 13. Do you distribute at least 85% of your annual net income or 3.5% of the aggregate fair market value of all of your nonexempt-use assets (whichever is greater) to your supported organization(s)? If "No," explain.

The best answer is "Yes" if that is the case. If "No," you have to explain.

Here is IRS guidance on this matter:

To satisfy the integral part test as a non-functionally integrated supporting organization, you must distribute at least 85% of your annual net income or 3.5% of the aggregate fair market value of all of your non-exempt-use assets (whichever is greater) to your supported organization(s). You can use Part V of Schedule A (Form 990 or 990-EZ) to help determine your answer to this question.

Schedule A is part of the annual tax-exempt information return filed with IRS.

Line 13a. How much do you contribute annually to each supported organization?

Give the total amount you give to each organization annually, and if there will be different amounts for different years, explain how you determine the amounts you will give.

Line 13b. What is the total annual revenue of each supported organization?

Give the total annual income of each organization you support. If you are giving to a certain program, list the total income to that program.

Line 13c. Do you or the supported organization(s) earmark your funds for support of a particular program or activity? If "Yes," explain.

If you are supporting specific activities or programs, answer "Yes" and give details of that support to those programs.

CHAPTER 28

SCHEDULE E

EFFECTIVE DATE

"One of the strongest characteristics of genius is the power of lighting its own fire."

—John W. Foster

If you have been in existence for more than 27 months, or your organization was automatically revoked for failure to file Form 990-series returns for three years, you have some special filing rules as far as effective date of your organization. You have to file Schedule E to determine the correct effective date.

Churches, organizations with gross revenue under $5,000 a year, organizations formed before 1969, or if you can prove you acted in good faith and that if IRS granted the earlier date, it would not prejudice the interests of the government, can get an earlier effective date.

If it is determined that you do not qualify for 501(c) (3) status from date of formation, you may still qualify for 501(c) (4) status for the dates between formation and filing the Form 1023. Normally donations are not deductible for periods covered under 501(c) (4) status.

WISCONSIN

Line 1. Are you applying for reinstatement of exemption after being automatically revoked for failure to file required returns or notices for three consecutive years? If "No," continue to Line 2.

If you have not been revoked for failure to file tax returns, answer "No" and go to the next question.

If you answer "Yes" because you have been revoked for failure to file tax returns for three years, you must select from the following choices for reinstatement:

1a. Revenue Procedure 2014-11, 2014-1 C.B. 411, provides procedures for reinstating your tax-exempt status. Select the section of Revenue Procedure 2014-11 under which you want us to consider your reinstatement request.

Section 4. You are seeking retroactive reinstatement under section 4 of Revenue Procedure 2014-11. By selecting this line, you attest that you meet the specified requirements of section 4, that your failure to file was not intentional, and that you have put in place procedures to file required returns or notices in the future. Do not complete the rest of Schedule E.

You are eligible for Section 4 if you could have filed Form 990-EZ or Form 990-N (meaning your revenues were under $200,000, and you just didn't file for whatever reason, this is your first time being automatically revoked for failure to file tax returns, and you are asking IRS to reinstate you within 15 months of being revoked). This is the easiest reinstatement. Basically you are telling IRS you are sorry you didn't file, you won't do it again, and that you have assigned a board member or other responsible person to keep up with it in the future so it doesn't happen again. Foundations cannot claim Section 4 because they cannot file Forms 990-EZ or 990-N. they must file Form 990-PF.

Section 5. You are seeking retroactive reinstatement under section 5 of Revenue Procedure 2014-11. By selecting this line, you attest that you meet the specified requirements of section 5, that you have filed required annual returns, that your failure to file was not intentional, and that you have put in place procedures to file required returns or notices in the future.

Describe how you exercised ordinary business care and prudence in determining and attempting to comply with your filing requirements in at least one of the three years of revocation and the steps you have taken or will take to avoid or mitigate future failures to file timely returns or notices. Do not complete the rest of Schedule E.

If it is more than 15 months since you appeared on the revoked list and you have filed the missing tax returns, you must tell IRS why you failed to file and what you plan to do to keep it from happening again in the future. Provide:

- A detailed statement of all the facts surrounding repeated failure to file for the three-year period.
- What circumstances led to continual failure, discovery of failure, and what you did to stop or lessen the consequences of the failure to file.
- You must address what you are doing now to keep this from happening again. You can add the task of filing the appropriate return to the job description of one of the board positions such as secretary or treasurer to make sure it gets done and that there is a responsible person to carry out the task or follow up with a bookkeeper or accountant to see that it is done and filed on time in the future.

- You must provide proof that you exercised ordinary business care and prudence in determining and attempting to comply with reporting requirements under section 6033 for at least one year of the three-year period. IRS will consider all your evidence and determine if you meet the Reasonable Cause Standard. Here are some things they consider that can lead to a favorable decision:

    - If you relied on written information from IRS that was in error
    - Events beyond your control that caused you not to be able to file for each of the three years
    - Acting responsibly by taking steps to avoid the failure to file and to keep it from happening in the future by trying to prevent the failure if it was foreseen; removing the problem that caused you not to file as soon as you became aware of the failure to file; putting policies and safeguards in place to make sure it doesn't happen in the future
    - A history of complying with filing and other requirements before and after the three-year period
    - How heavily you rely on volunteers to perform organizational activities also plays a part in the decision-making process. The more volunteers, the easier IRS will be on you about getting reinstated.
    - IRS has accepted the statement that the board members thought they didn't have to file tax returns until they reached $50,000 annual revenues. I have heard that from accountants and bookkeepers for years, so know that wrong advise is given all the time. If you are a victim of bad advise you counted on from a professional you trusted, that is a good enough reason to reinstate you.
    - If you want retroactive coverage of tax-exempt status, you need to be very thorough in your explanation

of what happened and make sure you let IRS know that you did not fail to comply as a rebellion against the tax system. You may even want to start your explanation with that statement so IRS gets the idea immediately that you were not rebellious. If your request for retroactive status is turned down, the date of your new Form 1023 filing will be the effective date for tax-exempt status.

You will not be revoked a second time unless you fail to file for three years AFTER receiving the new determination letter reinstating your tax-exempt status.

Section 6. You are seeking retroactive reinstatement under section 6 of Revenue Procedure 2014-11. By selecting this line, you attest that you meet the specified requirements of section 6, that you have filed required annual returns, that your failure to file was not intentional, and that you have put in place procedures to file required returns or notices in the future.

Section 6 is a choice if it has been more than 15 months since your organization appeared on the revocation list at IRS. You must have filed the missing tax returns and set up procedures to make sure it doesn't happen again.

IRS guidance on Section 6 includes:

Describe how you exercised ordinary business care and prudence in determining and attempting to comply with your filing requirements in each of the 3 years of revocation. Include a detailed explanation of all the facts and circumstances that led to the failure, the discovery of the failure, and the steps you have taken or will take to avoid or mitigate future failures to file timely returns or notices.

Section 7. You are seeking reinstatement under section 7 of Revenue Procedure 2014-11, effective the date you are filling this application. Do not complete the rest of Schedule E.

If you are just going to start over with a new 501(c)(3) effective date, mark this answer and stop here on Schedule E.

Line 2. Generally, if you did not file Form 1023 within 27 months of formation, the effective date of your exempt status will be the date you filed Form 1023 (submission date). Requests for an earlier effective date may be granted when there is evidence to establish you acted reasonably and in good faith and the grant of relief will not prejudice the interests of the government.

You have two choices:

- **Check this box if you accept the submission date as the effective date of your exempt status. Do not complete the rest of Schedule E.**
- **Check this box if you are requesting an earlier effective date than the submission date.**

Line 2a. Explain why you did not file Form 1023 within 27 months of formation, how you acted reasonably and in good faith, and how granting an earlier effective date will not prejudice the interests of the Government.

You may want to include the events that led to the failure to timely file Form 1023 and to the discovery of the failure, any reliance on the advice of a qualified tax professional and a description of the engagement and responsibilities of the professional as well as the extent to which you relied on the professional, a comparison of (1) what your aggregate tax liability would be if you had filed this application within the 27-month period with (2) what your aggregate liability would be if you were exempt as of your formation date, or any other information you believe will support your request for relief.

CHAPTER 29

SCHEDULE F

LOW-INCOME HOUSING

"Winners never quit, and quitters never win."
—Vince Lombardi

If you provide homes for low-income individuals (including elderly), you must provide affordable housing to a "significant segment" of low-income individuals in the community. That doesn't mean you have to have a bunch of houses; it means you must make whatever housing you have available to a "significant segment" of low-income people who need it. Don't play favorites or be narrow in focus.

Section 1: General Information

Line 1. Describe each facility including the type of facility, whether you own or lease the facility, how many residents it can accommodate, the current number of residents, and whether the residents purchase or rent housing from you.

Describe the type of housing you are providing (for example apartments, condos, co-ops, private residences). Give the maximum capacity of units, how many are currently occupied by residents, and the arrangement (rent or buy) you have with the occupants.

Line 2. Describe who qualifies for your housing in terms of income levels or other criteria and explain how you select residents.

Here are some HUD standards you can adopt if you do not already have criteria in place:

Eligibility based on:

1. *annual gross income;*
2. *whether qualified as elderly, a person with a disability, or as a family; and*
3. *U.S. citizenship or eligible immigration status.*

If eligible, we check references to make sure individuals and families will be good tenants. We deny admission to any applicant whose habits and practices may be expected to have a detrimental effect on other tenants or on the project's environment. We use income limits developed by HUD. HUD sets the lower income limits at 80% and very low income limits at 50% of the median income for the area.

Line 3. Do you meet the safe harbor requirements outlined in Revenue Procedure 96-32, 1996-1 C.B. 717, which provides guidelines for providing low-income housing that will be treated as charitable, including for each project that (a) at least 75 percent of the units are occupied by residents that qualify as low-income and (b) either at least 20 percent of the units are occupied by residents that also meet the very low-income limit for the area or 40 percent of the units are occupied by residents that also do not exceed 120 percent of the area's very low-income limit, and less than 25 percent of the units are provided at market rates to persons who have incomes in excess of the low-income limit?

The correct answer is "Yes."

IRS gives this guidance at *http://www.irs.gov/pub/irs-tege/rp_1996-32.pdf*

Revenue Procedure 96-32, 1996-1 C.B. 717 provides guidelines for providing low-income housing that will be treated as charitable. (At least 75% of the units are occupied by low-income tenants or 40% are occupied by tenants earning not more than 120% of the very low-income levels for the area.)

Line 4. Is your housing affordable to low-income residents? If "Yes," describe how your housing is made affordable to low-income residents.

Here are some HUD guidelines you can use if you do not already have a formula in place:

> *Rent would be based on a family's anticipated gross annual income less deductions, if any. We would exclude from annual income the following allowances: $480 for each dependent; $400 for any elderly family, or a person with a disability; and some medical deductions for families headed by an elderly person or a person with disabilities. Annual income is the anticipated total income from all sources received from the family head and spouse, and each additional member of the family 18 years of age or older.*

Line 5. Do you impose any restrictions to make sure that your housing remains affordable to low-income residents? If "Yes," describe these restrictions.

List your restrictions, if any.

Line 6. In addition to rent or mortgage payments, do residents pay periodic fees or maintenance charges? If "Yes," describe what these charges cover and how they are determined.

Are there any other fees? How are they determined? Give a detailed explanation.

Line 7. Do you provide social services to residents? If "Yes," describe these services.

Describe any social services provided.

Line 8. Do you participate in any government housing programs? If "Yes," describe these programs.

If you participate in Section 8 or any other federal, state, or local government housing programs, list and describe them.

CHAPTER 30

SCHEDULE G

SUCCESSORS TO OTHER ORGANIZATIONS

"Motivation is simple. You eliminate those who are not motivated."

—Lou Holtz

The main reason for this schedule is to make sure that no private benefit to shareholders or individuals occurs when one organization (the predecessor) is taken over by or converted to another organization, even if the predecessor was not a tax-exempt organization.

IRS guidance on this schedule includes:

> You should consider this schedule as a **successor** organization if any of the following situations pertain to you.
>
> - You took or will take over activities previously conducted by another organization.
> - You took or will take over 25% or more of the **fair market value** of the net assets of another organization.

- *You were established upon the conversion of an organization from **for-profit** to non-profit status.*

The other organization is the **predecessor** organization. You should complete this schedule regardless of whether the predecessor (other organization) was exempt or not exempt from federal income tax.

For purposes of this schedule, a *"for-profit"* organization is one in which persons are permitted to have an ownership or partnership interest, such as corporate stock. It includes sole proprietorships, corporations, and other entities that provide for ownership interests.

Line 1. List the name, last address, and EIN of your predecessor organization and describe its activities.

Give the name, Federal Employer Identification Number, and address of the predecessor organization.

Line 2. List the owners, partners, principal stockholders, officers, and governing board members of your predecessor organization. Include their names, addresses, and share/interest in the predecessor organization (if for-profit).

Provide all requested details about the previous organization.

Line 3. Are you a successor to a for-profit organization? If "Yes," explain your relationship with the predecessor organization that resulted in your creation and explain why you took over the activities or assets of a for-profit organization or converted from for-profit to nonprofit status; continue to Line 4.

Provide all requested information about why you took over the organization and its assets. Be detailed and specific.

Line 3a. Explain your relationship with the other organization that resulted in your creation and why you took over the activities or assets of another organization.

Provide all requested information giving as much detail as possible.

Line 4. Do or will you maintain a working relationship with any of the persons listed in question 2 or with any for-profit organization in which these persons own more than a 35% interest? If "Yes," describe the relationship.

Answer the question as accurately as possible based on the information you have and the agreement you have reached with the predecessor organization.

Line 5. Were any assets transferred, whether by gift or sale, from the predecessor organization to you? If "Yes," provide a list of assets, indicate the value of each asset, explain how the value was determined, and attach an appraisal, if available. For each asset listed, also explain if the transfer was by gift, sale, or combination thereof and describe any restrictions that were placed on the use or sale of the assets.

List the assets you received, the nature of the transfer (gift or sale), whether the assets were restricted in use, and the value if known or if you have an appraisal.

Line 6. Were any debts or liabilities transferred from the predecessor for-profit organization to you? If "Yes," provide a list of the debts or liabilities that were transferred to you, indicating the amount of each, how the amount was determined, and the name of the person to whom the debt or liability is owed.

List the debts, amounts, how determined (such as existing balance at time of transfer), and who is owed.

Line 7. Will you lease or rent any property or equipment to or from the predecessor organization or any persons listed in Line 2 or a for-profit organization in which these persons own more than a 35% interest? If "Yes," describe the arrangement(s) including how the lease or rental value was determined.

Explain any lease or rental agreements with the predecessor.

CHAPTER 31

SCHEDULE H

ORGANIZATIONS PROVIDING SCHOLARSHIPS, FELLOWSHIPS, EDUCATIONAL LOANS, OR OTHER EDUCATIONAL GRANTS TO INDIVIDUALS AND PRIVATE FOUNDATIONS REQUESTING ADVANCE APPROVAL OF INDIVIDUAL GRANT PROCEDURES

"A year from now you may wish you had started today."

—Karen Lamb

IRS wants to make sure that any scholarships you give as a tax-exempt organization are fair in terms of nondiscrimination, merit or need, and available to an open-ended group instead of a preselected group. The scholarship is tax-free to the recipient if he or she is a degree-seeking candidate and uses the funds for educational expenses that include tuition, fees, books, supplies, and equipment for courses. Acceptable educational expenses do not include room, board, travel, research, clerical help, and equipment not required for a course of study.

Section 1: Public charities and private foundations complete lines 1 through 8 of this section

Line 1. Describe the types of educational grants you provide to individuals, such as scholarships, fellowships, loans, etc., including the purpose, number and amount(s) of grants, how the program is publicized, and if you award educational loans, the terms of the loans.

Provide a full explanation of grants, loans, and scholarships provided. If you do not have all the details determined yet, say so.

IRS guidance on this question includes:

- *If you conduct more than one grant program, describe each program separately.*
- *If you make educational loans, describe the terms of the loan (for example, the factors you consider in selecting or approving loan recipients, interest rate, duration, forgiveness provision, etc.). Also, describe whether any financial institutions or other lenders are involved in your program.*
- *Explain how you will publicize your program and whether you publicize to the general public or to another group of possible recipients. Include specific information about the geographic area in which your program will be publicized and the means you will use, such as through newspaper advertisements, school district announcements, or community groups.*

Line 2. Do you maintain case histories showing recipients of your scholarships, fellowships, educational loans, or other educational grants, including names, addresses, purposes of awards, amount of each grant, manner of selection, and relationship (if any) to officers, trustees, or donors of funds to you? If "No," explain.

Do you keep complete records of who gets scholarships, grants, loans, etc.? Describe the records you keep. More information is found in Revenue Rulings 56-304 1956-2 C.B. 306. If you do not keep records, you must explain how you will make sure your program meets exempt purposes.

The correct answer is "Yes."

Line 3. Describe the specific criteria you use to determine who is eligible for your program (for example, eligibility selection criteria could consist of graduating high school students from a particular high school who will attend college, writers of scholarly works about American history, etc.).

Who is eligible? What is the criteria?

Line 4. Describe the specific criteria you use to select recipients (for example, specific selection criteria could consist of prior academic performance, financial need, etc.).

How you will select recipients, number of recipients, the amount for each recipient, and any requirements (such as grade point average) the recipients must meet.

Line 5. Describe any requirement or condition you impose on recipients to obtain, maintain, or qualify for renewal of a grant (for example, specific requirements or conditions could consist of attendance at a four-year college, maintaining a certain grade point average, teaching in public school after graduation from college, etc.).

If you plan to give renewal grants, explain how you will determine that the recipient has met the requirements for additional educational assistance.

Line 6. Describe your procedures for supervising the scholarships, fellowships, educational loans, or other educational grants. Explain whether you obtain reports and grade transcripts from recipients, or you pay grants directly to a school under an arrangement whereby the school will apply the grant funds only for enrolled students who are in good standing. Also, describe your procedures for taking action if the terms of the award are violated.

It is a good idea to pay the school directly with instructions to apply the funds only to enrolled students in good standing. If your selected recipient is not in good standing because of grades, attendance, etc., then funds will be withheld. Describe how you will manage your grants to ensure the funds are not being wasted or misused. Also explain your plan of action if the terms of the scholarship or fellowship, etc. are violated.

Line 7. How do you determine who is on the selection committee for the awards made under your program?

Who is on the current selection committee, what are the requirements, and how do you replace selection committee members? Selection can be made by board members, community members, or a combination of the two.

Line 8. Are relatives of members of the selection committee, or of your officers, directors, or substantial contributors eligible for awards made under your program? If "Yes," what measures do you take to ensure unbiased selections?

The best answer is "No." Are family members of your selection committee eligible? If so, how do you remain unbiased in selection? Private foundations are not allowed to award to disqualified persons.

Section 2: Private foundations complete lines 1 through 7 of this section. Public charities do not complete this section.

Line 1. As a private foundation, do you want this application to be considered as a request for advance approval of grant making procedures? If "No," do not complete the rest of Schedule H.

IRS guidance for this question includes:

- *Answer "Yes," if you're a private foundation and you're requesting advance approval of your grant-making procedures under section 4945(g).*
- *Answer "No," if you're a private foundation but don't wish to request advance approval of your grant-making procedures under section 4945(g). If you answer "No" the amounts you distribute as educational grants provided to individuals may be considered taxable expenditures under section 4945.*

  For more information about advance approval of grant-making procedures of a private foundation, go to IRS.gov/charities-non-profit/private-foundations/advance-approval-of-grant-makingprocedures.

WISCONSIN

Line 1a. Check the box(es) indicating under which section(s) you want your grant making procedures to be considered.

4945(g)(1) - Scholarship or fellowship grant to an individual for study at an educational institution

4945(g)(3) - Other grants, including loans, to an individual for travel, study, or other similar purposes, to enhance a particular skill of the grantee or to produce a specific product

IRS guidance on this question includes:

- *Check the box for section "4945(g)(1)" if your award qualifies as a scholarship or fellowship grant that's awarded on an objective and nondiscriminatory basis and is used for study at a school (see Schedule B for what is considered a school).*
- *Check the box for "4945(g)(3)" if the purpose of your award is to achieve a specific objective, produce a report or other similar product, or improve or enhance a literary, artistic, musical, scientific, teaching, or other similar capacity, skill, or talent of the recipient. Include your educational loan program under this section.*
- *You may check more than one box.*

Line 2. Do you represent that you will (1) arrange to receive and review grantee reports annually and upon completion of the purpose for which the grant was awarded, (2) investigate diversions of funds from their intended purposes, and (3) take all reasonable and appropriate steps to recover diverted funds, ensure other grant funds held by a grantee are used for their intended purposes, and withhold further payments to grantees until you obtain grantees' assurances that future diversions will not occur and that grantees will take extraordinary precautions to prevent future diversions from occurring?

The correct answer is "Yes."

Line 3. Do you represent that you will maintain all records relating to individual grants, including information obtained to evaluate grantees, identify whether a grantee is a disqualified person, establish the amount and purpose of each grant, and establish that you undertook the supervision and investigation of grants described in Line 2?

The correct answer is "Yes."

Line 4. Do you or will you award scholarships, fellowships, and educational loans to attend an educational institution based on the status of an individual being an employee of a particular employer? If "No," do not complete the rest of Schedule H.

Self-explanatory.

Line 5. Will you comply with the seven conditions and either the percentage tests or facts and circumstances test for scholarships, fellowships, and educational loans to attend an educational institution as set forth in Revenue Procedures 76-47, 1976-2 C.B. 670, and 80-39, 1980-2 C.B. 772, which apply to inducement, selection committee, eligibility requirements, objective basis of selection, employment, course of study, and other objectives?

The correct answer is "Yes."

Line 6. Do you or will you provide scholarships, fellowships, or educational loans to attend an educational institution to employees of a particular employer? If "No," continue to Line 7.

Self-explanatory.

Line 6a. Will you award grants to 10% or fewer of the eligible applicants who were actually considered by the selection committee in selecting recipients of grants in that year as provided by Revenue Procedures 76-47 and 80-39?

Revenue Procedure 76-47 has to do with educational grants (e.g. – scholarships and fellowships).

Revenue Procedure 80-39 has to do with educational loans.

The correct answer is "Yes."

Line 7. Do you provide scholarships, fellowships, or educational loans to attend an educational institution to children of employees of a particular employer? If "No," do not complete the rest of Schedule H.

Self-explanatory. This question also includes family members, not just children.

Line 7a. Will you award grants to 25% or fewer of the eligible applicants who were actually considered by the selection committee in selecting recipients of grants in that year as provided by Revenue Procedures 76-47 and 80-39? If "Yes," do not complete the rest of Schedule H.

Those two Revenue Procedures also address eligibility of grants to children of employees of a particular employer. The correct answer is "Yes."

Line 7b. Will you award grants to 10% or fewer of the number of employees' children who can be shown to be eligible for grants (whether or not they submitted an application) in that year, as provided by Revenue Procedures 76-47 and 80-39? If "Yes," describe how you will determine who can be shown to be eligible for grants without submitting an application, such as by obtaining written statements or other information about the expectations of employees' children to attend an educational institution; do not complete the rest of Schedule H.

The correct answer is "Yes." You must determine how you will come up with the numbers of eligible employees' children so you can tell if you have awarded 10% or less.

WISCONSIN

Line 7c. Will you award grants based on facts and circumstances that demonstrate that the grants will not be considered compensation for past, present, or future services or otherwise provide a significant benefit to the particular employer? If "Yes," describe the facts and circumstances you believe will demonstrate that the grants are neither compensatory nor a significant benefit to the particular employer. In your explanation, describe why you cannot satisfy either the 25% test or the 10% test in questions 7a and 7b.

The easy answer is "No." If you must answer "Yes," you will need to explain how you will comply with Revenue Procedures 76-47 and 80-39.

PART IV
FORM 1023-EZ

CHAPTER 32

FORM 1023-EZ

STREAMLINED APPLICATION

*"You are what you think.
You are what you go for.
You are what you do!"*

—Bob Richards

On July 1, 2014, IRS added Form 1023-EZ, *Streamlined Application for Recognition of Exemption under Section 501(c) (3) of the Internal Revenue Code*. IRS has revised the application a few times since, and at the time of publication, the latest form is from October 2018. This new way of filing is for smaller organizations and is designed to speed up approval and cut the paperwork down to manageable. It must be filed online, the cost is $275, and you must complete the Eligibility Checklist (which is 5 pages long but not difficult). This is great news for small nonprofits because the Form 1023-EZ is only three pages compared to the Form 1023, which is 18 pages, plus 22 more pages of schedules. Eligibility worksheet is located in the instruction package for Form 1023-EZ. There are many restrictions on the use of this new form, and many types of nonprofits are not eligible.

WISCONSIN

To be eligible to use the Form 1023-EZ, you must meet ALL these requirements:

1. Have or project less than $50,000 gross receipts for the past three years and projected for the next three years
2. Have less than $250,000 in assets
3. Be formed in the U. S. and have a U. S. mailing address (or U. S. territory)
4. Must not be a successor to, or controlled by, an entity suspended under Section 501(p) terrorist organization
5. Cannot be a limited liability corporation (LLC)
6. Cannot be successor to a for-profit entity
7. Must not be a church, convention, or association of churches
8. Must not be a school, college, university, or cooperative service organization for an educational institution
9. Must not be a hospital, medical research organization, or cooperative hospital service organization
10. Must not be an agricultural research organization
11. Must not be a qualified charitable risk pool
12. Must not be a supporting organization to other nonprofits
13. Must not be providing credit counseling or consumer credit services
14. Cannot invest 5% or more of your total assets in securities or funds that are not publicly traded
15. Must not participate, or intend to participate, in partnerships (including entities treated as partnerships for federal tax purposes) in which you share profits and losses with partners other than section 501(c) (3) organizations
16. Cannot sell carbon credits or carbon offsets
17. Must not be an HMO
18. Cannot engage in Accountable Care Organization (ACO) activities
19. Cannot maintain donor-advised funds
20. Cannot be testing for public safety
21. Must not be a private operating foundation

Here is a rundown of the sections of Form 1023-EZ with comments to help you answer the questions:

Part 1: Identification of Applicant

The new form combines Part I and Part V of Form 1023 but eliminates many questions. It is much faster to fill out than the long form. List up to five board members. Email address is optional. List website if yours is up and running. If it is in work or not ready yet, leave it off. IRS sometimes sends a request for copies of the web pages if you have a website listed, which can hold up your application approval.

Part II: Organizational Structure

Most organizations will be corporations, and the organizing document is the Articles of Incorporation. It is possible and perfectly acceptable to be incorporated in one state, and have your mailing address in another. That is not the norm, but it is okay if that describes your organization. Just be sure to put the incorporation state in this section. You must be able to check the boxes for questions 5, 6, and 7. If you cannot, you will not be approved for 501(c)(3) tax-exempt status.

Part III: Your Specific Activities

Line 1: Briefly describe the organization's mission or most significant activities (limit 250 characters)

You may have to condense a long mission statement to make it fit in this box. Go to the first page of your bylaws and find your mission and condense it to fit 250 characters.

Line 2. Enter the appropriate 3-character NTEE Code that best describes your activities.

NTEE Code is a 3-character code that describes your activities. A list of NTEE codes can be found on pages 21 – 23 of the Form 1023-EZ instructions, which are located online at *https://www.irs.gov/pub/irs-pdf/i1023ez.pdf*

Common NTEE codes include:

P80: Services to Promote the Independence of Specific Populations

X20: Christian

A99: Arts, Culture, and Humanities

D20: Animal Protection and Welfare

F20: Alcohol, Drug and Substance Abuse, Dependency Prevention, and Treatment

I72: Prevention of Child Abuse

O50: Youth Development Programs

There are many NTEE codes. Check them out to find the one that best fits your organization. We suggest you stay away from the codes that start with the letter Y. They are mutual benefit organization codes and do not qualify for 501(c) (3) public charity status.

Line 3. To qualify for exemption as a section 501(c) (3) organization, you must be organized and operated exclusively to further one or more of the following purposes. By checking the box or boxes below, you attest that you are organized and operated exclusively to further the purposes indicated. Check all that apply.

Most organizations are charitable. Remember that you are not eligible to use Form 1023-EZ if you are a school or church organization, or test for public safety.

Line 4. You must be able to check the box attesting that you will not violate the rules.

Lines 5 - 12: If you cannot answer all these questions "No," file the long form to avoid delays and follow-up with IRS because they are going to need much more information to approve you, especially if you are working outside the United States.

Part IV: Foundation Classification

Line 1. Are you applying for recognition as a church, school, or hospital (described in section 170(b)(1)(A)(i), (ii), or (iii) of the Internal Revenue Code)? If yes, stop. Do not file Form 1023-EZ. See Instructions

You must mark "No" to continue with this form.

Line 2. If you qualify for public charity status, check the appropriate box (2a - 2c below) and skip to Part V below.

- Check 2a if your organization will get most of its revenues from donations and grants.

- Check 2b if your organization will get most of its revenues from membership fees and/or program services fees.
- Organizations that qualify under 2c normally file the long form.

Line 3. If you are not described in items 2a - 2c above, you are a private foundation. As a private foundation, you are required by section 508(e) to have specific provisions in your organizing document, unless you rely on the operation of state law in the state in which you were formed to meet these requirements. These specific provisions require that you operate to avoid liability for private foundation excise taxes under sections 4941-4945. Select this box to attest that your organizing document contains the provisions required by section 508(e) or that your organizing document does not need to include the provisions required by section 508(e) because you rely on the operation of state law in your particular state to meet the requirements of section 508(e). (See the instructions for explanation of the section 508(e) requirements.)

Select this option (Instead of 2a, b, or c) if you are a foundation. Your requirements will be much different from public charities, your tax returns much longer, and the rules will be harder to live with. In addition, you organizing document (Articles of Incorporation by whatever name your state calls it) must contain the following:

As a private foundation, we meet IRS requirement for foundations in addition to 501(c) (3) requirements:

1. *The corporation will distribute its income for each tax year at a time and in a manner as not to become subject to the tax on undistributed income imposed by section 4942 of the Internal Revenue Code, or the corresponding section of any future federal tax code.*

2. The corporation won't engage in any act of self-dealing as defined in section 4941(d) of the Internal Revenue Code, or the corresponding section of any future federal tax code.
3. The corporation won't retain any excess business holdings as defined in section 4943(c) of the Internal Revenue Code, or the corresponding section of any future federal tax code.
4. The corporation won't make any investments in a manner as to subject it to tax under section 4944 of the Internal Revenue Code, or the corresponding section of any future federal tax code.
5. The corporation won't make any taxable expenditures as defined in section 4945(d) of the Internal Revenue Code, or the corresponding section of any future federal tax code.

If you meet the requirement by relying on state law, you can mark this choice in good conscience. See Appendix B at the end of this book for a list of states and their rules for you to be able to rely on state law for foundation requirements.

Part V: Reinstatement After Automatic Revocation

Box 1: When you check the box, you are saying you did not fail to file intentionally, and that you have made changes to keep it from happening again.
Box 2: You are seeking reinstatement effective the date IRS processes this application instead of the revocation date.

There are three conditions you must meet to use this form for reinstatement: It must be the first time you were revoked, you must have been eligible to file Form 990-N (electronic postcard return) or Form 990-EZ (short form return), and you must file within 15 months of being revoked.

HOW TO FILE FORM 1023-EZ

Go to *www.pay.gov* and register. Enter 1023-EZ in the search box and complete the form. You can set up a deduction from your bank account or use a credit or debit card to pay the application fee.

Not everyone is eligible to file the Form 1023-EZ and not everyone should that is eligible. If you cannot use the Form 1023-EZ, you will need to use the long form, Form 1023.

PART V
SPECIAL FEATURE BY GRANT GURU JUDY HANNA

CHAPTER 33

THE ART OF GRANT WRITING FOR YOUR NONPROFIT

By Grant Guru JUDY HANNA

"Like the magic of creating a painting, successful grant writing must capture the combination of skill, creativity, passion, and focus. It's an intoxicating combination once you master the ability to skillfully navigate the diverse offerings and hold that first grant award close to your heart."

—JUDY HANNA

Every grant writer is a novice in the beginning and, as with all adventures, learning how to present your written proposal is key to reaping the coveted benefits. I once was a novice myself, but with years of practice, stepping in mud holes, and dusting myself off after repeated rejections, I grew into the process as a seasoned, successful grant writer with a good track record. I would like to share some common missteps in the grant writing process to help you avoid costly mistakes and enhance your outcomes for funding.

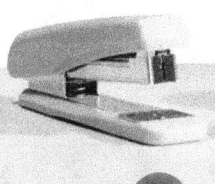

HOW TO AVOID MUD HOLES AND ACHIEVE GREATER REWARDS

FOCUS

Your mission statement is your focus, the driving force for how you will begin your journey to locate available grants. Below, you will find two sample mission statements. Mission statements are always one statement ranging from one line to five lines.

MISSION STATEMENT FOR EDUCATION AND ADVOCACY: To provide accessible, integrated awareness education and advocacy to senior citizens to enhance quality of life, autonomy, health, safety, and economic well-being, thereby empowering them to live on their own terms independently in their own communities with respect, dignity, and equality

MISSION STATEMENT FOR HUNGER: To prepare healthy snacks to pack into weekend backpacks for latchkey kids

RESEARCH

Overwhelming might be a fine term to describe the massive number of corporate, state, federal, foundation, and private grant offerings. To provide you with one example, over 86,700 foundations exist in the United States with reported annual funding exceeding $60 billion, or in visual terms, $60,244,456,505. That number represents foundations that offer funding and does not include the massive number of funding outlets granting awardees through state and federal governmental, private, and organizational giving.

So, where do you begin? The step-by-step process below will provide some guidance and a lifeline to keep you afloat and on the right track for funding your projects.

WHO ARE YOU SERVING?

Revisit your mission statement. Who are you helping through your nonprofit? Let's suppose you are helping elderly with critical needs that aren't covered through other avenues, and the small $800 monthly Social Security check barely covers their utilities and medication. Seniors often are forced to choose between buying food or repairing a rusted-out air conditioning unit, so searching for funding to assist them based on critical needs you have noted would broaden the search to include major corporate foundations such as Home Depot Foundation where new air conditioning units can be secured.

WHY DOES YOUR NONPROFIT EXIST?

Before you begin writing any grant, you must have fact-based knowledge regarding the needs of those you intend to serve through your nonprofit. You must assemble your research to effectively explain why your chosen target groups of underserved people need your help, what they need, and why you exist. Some things to consider:

    a. Do you have surveys from your target group?
    b. Do you have sourced data from your research as to why you need to help?
    c. Do you have media articles?
    d. Do you have a target radius?
    e. How broad is your scope of help?

f. Do you have a reliable number of approximately how many will be served?

g. Do you have a list of ways in which you will help based on the needs?

WHY DO YOU NEED THIS INFORMATION?

One of the most common mud holes stepped in by novice grant writers is caused by a lack of research on the focus, impact, and outcomes you project for your charity. Funding sources will not fund an organization that can't justify their existence with clear and concise proof of specific needs to be addressed.

HOW DO YOU PLAN TO REACH YOUR TARGET AUDIENCE?

a. Do you have a plan of action?
b. Do you have a core group to help with your project?
c. Do you have a network in place to help you reach your goals?
d. Do you have contact information for your target group?
e. How will you conduct your awareness campaign?
f. How will you be contacted for help?
g. Do you have presentation materials that define your focus?
h. Do you have a marketing strategy?
i. How will you publicize any grants you receive?

WHY ARE THE ANSWERS IMPORTANT?

Funding agents want to know that your group is on solid ground with a well-crafted set of tools to ensure that people who need help can contact you. It is important to have a network in place with similar organizations, news media, materials, speaking engagements, and a referral base. All major funding outlets want to know that your commitment to what you propose is worth the honor of handing money over to you.

HOW ARE YOU DIFFERENT?

It is important to show a funding source that you are simply not duplicating services already in place for your target group. Prepare information that clearly shows what is available and what is not. By doing this, you assure the funding source that you are not reinventing the wheel, but are instead offering a service that is deficient or fully lacking for your target group. Research every organization or group that offers assistance to your target group, and define the differences or lack of available assistance.

BEING DIFFERENT IS GOOD IN THE GRANT WORLD

Funding sources do not want to fund an organization that is simply a spinoff of another organization with highly similar well-organized methodology.

THE PROCESS BEGINS

Now you can begin the Internet search for available grants. I suggest that grant writers first search what is available in their own state for nonprofits like yours. We go back to our example of helping elderly. Your search should begin with this broad information: "Funding grants for elderly." That search will display page after page of possible grants available to serve the needs of elderly. Then you will need to weed out those grants that do not apply to your mission statement.

Beware of the hype ads that ask you to pay for information. Do not step in that mud hole. There are unscrupulous scammers who constantly push "free" grants but want you to send money for the information you seek. Information for legitimate outlets is available, and if you are willing to take the time to search them out, your only cost to find what you are looking for is your investment of time.

ARE YOU ELIGIBLE?

Every grant listing has criteria attached. A funding source in Oklahoma may only serve needs in Oklahoma, Texas, and New Mexico, so if you are in Tennessee, you will not want to step in another known mud hole and write a grant to a funding source that clearly does not serve your state. Most grants exclude funding for individuals, private organizations (you are a public charity, not a private organization), building projects, operational funds, and fundraisers.

READ THE GRANT CRITERIA

Once you have located available grants that fit the mission of your organization and you are eligible, then carefully read the criteria for submitting. You will find that some grantors have short windows for applications and will not review if sent outside of the stated open submission dates. Stay within those dates when you submit.

Pay attention to the following instructions you will face:

a. Some grantors have their own form that must be submitted

b. Most grantors provide an outline of information needed from your organization
c. Some grantors require a query letter before submission
d. Some grantors require that your organization carry a $1 million insurance policy
e. Some grantors require your organization to be in operation for two years before submitting a proposal
f. Most major grantors require a recently completed audit before considering a request from your group
g. All grantors require a copy of your nonprofit designation paperwork (determination letter, and sometimes articles of incorporation)
h. Some grantors require that your organization thank them publicly and provide proof of the announcement after a grant is awarded. Publicity is usually via newspaper, magazine or television.
i. Most government sources will post "request for proposals" for various types of offerings and every specific item requested must be addressed according to the guidelines posted for the request. Competition is fierce for government grants and a poorly written or researched grant will be rejected quickly.
j. Foundation and corporate grants often request online-only applications that must be uploaded to the foundation or corporate website. Read the criteria and assemble your information before heading into the application. Copy a set of the listed criteria and take the time to handwrite your responses and refine the information before inputting information into the actual application form.
k. Some outlets will only fund if you will allow them to see your books first.
l. Local funding sources are user-friendly and less intense on criteria, but only small amounts are generally provided to awardees.

CAPTIVATE YOUR FUNDING SOURCE

Capture the reader's attention immediately when writing a grant proposal. You hold the power to ensure that the grant source sees your heart and feels your determination. The grant proposal is your executive summary of sorts that grabs the interest and attention of the reader. It is your chance to compel the reader to continue reading. The passion, the brief data, and the strength of your plan will be highly evident when you define and explore the depth of the needs you will fulfill. A weak start is often a quick turn off, and your grant proposal joins thousands of other proposals in File 13 without a backward glance.

> You hold the power to ensure that the grant source sees your heart and feels your determination.

A PICTURE IS WORTH A THOUSAND WORDS

Providing a picture within your grant request is powerful. Visual learners inhabit the planet and are drawn to consume the meaning of photos incorporated in grants. If you are helping battered women, photos of battered women you know (with permission) are powerful. If you are helping provide backpacks with healthy food for children, the photos of children with the backpacks and the type of food you provide are compelling.

Document every activity you have within your organization with photos. They will come in handy when you decide to submit a grant request. Showing a funding source what you have done is one of the greatest tools you will bring to the table to substantiate your request and achieve higher attention levels for funding. Don't overdo it. Choose your photos with care, and don't utilize a large number of photos.

FOLLOW INSTRUCTIONS

The biggest mud hole in existence for grant writers is not following the instructions provided by the grantor. Read and reread every stated requirement for submission. Check and double-check your materials for compliance. If the grant source requires a cover letter and you fail to include one, it's over. A forgotten financial report, a summary that does not meet length requirements, or failure to include your website address are reasons for disqualification. Competition for grant money is fierce, and one small mistake will take you out of the running.

LANDING SMALL GRANTS VS. LARGE GRANTS

Smaller grants tend to be easier to secure, so don't dismiss the possibility of writing numerous small grants to businesses and corporations. Many small grant awards can add up quickly. Don't dismiss writing small one-page request grants to service organizations in your area. Those add up as well and generally range from $250-$1,000 per grant. Smaller grants do not normally require the intensive work that must go into larger grants. A federal or state grant may take more than two full months to write, but if you are focused on the process and have your ducks in a row, the payout can be massive. There are never guarantees that you will receive one thin dime from your efforts. The rejection letters can leave you feeling depressed and frustrated, especially when you worked so hard to craft a heartfelt submission. It's like anything you do in life; practice makes perfect. Try and try again because different readers with different perspectives are reviewing your work and request. A failed grant from one funding source may even pass muster with another.

> Many small grant awards can add up quickly.

AUTHORS' NOTE

Kitty has worked with Judy Hanna and she is one of the best grant writers she has ever known. Judy has seen great success as a large grant writer and presenter for over 25 years, provides custom designed grant writing workshops for groups, organizations, colleges, universities, and schools across the United States upon request, and provides grant writing services. If you are looking for a talented grant writer, look no further. She doesn't know we are including this, but for further information and quotes, email *hannajudy@icloud.com*

PART VI
SPECIAL CIRCUMSTANCES

CHAPTER 34

AUTOMATIC REVOCATION OF 501(C) (3) STATUS

"Confidence doesn't come out of nowhere. It's a result of something ... hours and days and weeks and years of constant work and dedication."

—Roger Staubach

Most tax-exempt organizations have to file an annual report with IRS. This report is some version of Form 990, and can be:

- Form 990, Return of Organization Exempt From Income Tax
- Form 990-EZ, Short Return of Organization Exempt From Income Tax
- Form 990-PF, Return of Private Foundation
- Form 990-N, Information e-Postcard

If you fail to file this return for three consecutive years, IRS takes away or revokes your tax-exempt status. This is called *Automatic Revocation* because the computer does it automatically and you are put on a list of organizations that no longer have tax-exempt status. That list can be found at *https://www.irs.gov/charities-non-profits/tax-exempt-organization-search*

If you have been automatically revoked, you must resubmit your entire application (including the required fee) and ask IRS to reinstate your tax-exempt status.

Normally the reinstatement date is the date of the new application to IRS, but there are some exceptions. For the date to be retroactive back to the date of revocation, you must file your application for reinstatement within 15 months of whichever is later:

- The date on the revocation letter from IRS
- The date IRS posted the revocation on their website

In addition, you must jump through some hoops to get the retroactive date. For example, IRS requires a detailed statement of all the facts surrounding repeated failure to file.

- What circumstances led to continual failure, discovery of failure, and what you did to stop or lessen the consequences of the failure to file.
- You must address what you are doing now to keep this from happening again. You can add the task of filing the appropriate return to the job description of one of the board positions such as secretary or treasurer to make sure it gets done and that there is a responsible person to carry out the task or follow up with a bookkeeper or accountant to see that it is done and filed on time in the future.
- Documentation and evidence of the explanations you gave to get retroactive reinstatement.
- All the missing returns for all the years a return was due (some form of Form 990-series return), including the three years not filed and the current year if applicable. If in doubt, contact IRS and ask them specifically what returns are due.
- You must provide proof that you exercised ordinary business care and prudence in determining and attempting

to comply with reporting requirements under section 6033 for at least one of the three years. IRS will consider all your evidence and determine if you meet the Reasonable Cause Standard. Here are some things they consider that can lead to a favorable decision:

- If you relied on written information from IRS that was in error
- Events beyond your control that caused you not to be able to file for each of the three years and the three-year period as a whole
- Acting responsibly by taking steps to avoid the failure to file and to keep it from happening in the future by trying to prevent the failure if it was foreseen; removing the problem that caused you not to file as soon as you became aware of the failure to file; putting policies and safeguards in place to make sure it doesn't happen in the future
- A history of complying with filing and other requirements before and after the three-year period
- How heavily you rely on volunteers to perform organizational activities also plays a part in the decision-making process. The more volunteers, the easier IRS will be on you about getting reinstated.

If you want retroactive coverage of tax-exempt status, you need to be very thorough in your explanation of what happened and make sure you let IRS know that you did not fail to comply as a rebellion against the tax system. If your request for retroactive status is turned down, the date of your new Form 1023 filing will be the effective date for tax-exempt status.

You will not be revoked a second time unless you fail to file for three years AFTER receiving the new determination letter reinstating your tax-exempt status.

PART VII
FOLLOW-UP TASKS

CHAPTER 35

ANNUAL FILING REQUIREMENTS WITH IRS

"It's not the size of the dog in the fight, but the size of the fight in the dog."
—Archie Griffin

REQUIRED ELECTRONIC FILING BY EXEMPT ORGANIZATIONS:

For tax years beginning on or after July 2, 2019, section 3101 of P. L. 116-25 requires that returns by exempt organizations be filed electronically.

In other words, nonprofit tax returns starting with fiscal years ending 2020 and after must be filed online. Paper returns will no longer be accepted.

IMPORTANT RULE: If you are a nonprofit, you must file an annual tax return *even if you have not applied for 501(c) (3) status yet*. The requirement is based on your organization having state nonprofit status, not on IRS granting 501(c) (3) status. Churches do not have to file annual returns.

The IRS gives you tax-exempt status, but with conditions. You must report to them annually (with very limited exceptions) about the income and expenses of the nonprofit organization. The form used to report depends on the status of the organization in terms of revenue, assets, and type of nonprofit. The smaller you are, the less you have to report. In most cases, if your income is less than $50,000, you do not even have to give an exact amount.

If you are a church or subordinate auxiliary of a church, you have no reporting requirements. However, many churches choose to report voluntarily to create transparency and keep everything on the up and up. Other organizations that do not have to file annual reports include state institutions and organizations that fall under parent organizations and qualify as auxiliary organizations of the parent. When in doubt, call IRS and ask. The number is 877-829-5500.

If you fail to file the required tax form for three years, your tax-exempt status will be automatically revoked the third year. At that time, you must reapply for tax-exempt status and pay the fee all over again. Consider assigning the responsibility of completing the required returns to a specific position on the board of directors or board of trustees so that it gets done on time every year. The person holding the assigned position should be responsible for reporting the progress, the completion, or problems to the board concerning the required filings. Being assigned to make sure it gets done is not the same as having to actually do the paperwork. An accountant or bookkeeper can do the return. It is the assigned board member's job to make sure it gets done and filed on time.

The reports you file with IRS are public records except that the name of the donors and the amount of their contributions are not public record. When filing, leave off social security numbers and other identifying information for the officers, directors, trustees, and other officials because the information given in the return is available to the public.

Filing a nonprofit tax return consists of completing some version of the IRS Form 990-series. The versions are similar to the Form 1040 series that individual taxpayers file in that there is a long form (Form 1040), short form (Form 1040A), and the simple, uncomplicated form (Form 1040EZ). The difference is that the Form 990-series is for nonprofits and there is no tax due; the filing is for information only.

Form 990
Return of Organization Exempt from Income Tax

This is the long form that must be filed if an organization's assets are over $500,000 or their annual revenue from all sources is over $200,000. It applies to all Section 501(c), 527, or 4947(a)(1) organizations except black lung benefit trusts and private foundations. The long form is similar to a tax return for an individual with a business. Just like an individual tax return, not everything on the form applies to everyone filing the return. Also, depending on the nature of the business, extra schedules may be required. A nonprofit organization may be required to file extra schedules depending on the nature of the nonprofit endeavors, interaction with other organizations, types of fundraising, political activity, compensation, operations outside the United States, major donors, and other considerations.

Form 990-EZ
Short Form Return of Organization Exempt from Income Tax

This is the short form that may be filed if an organization's assets are under $500,000 and their income is less than $200,000. The exceptions are sponsoring organizations of donor-advised funds, organizations that operate one or more hospital facilities, and certain controlling organizations defined in Section 512(b)(13). They must file Form 990.

Form 990-N
E-Postcard

Most smaller organizations with 501(c)(3) tax-exempt approval and income under $50,000 can file the Form 990-N, but can also file the Form 990-EZ or Form 990 if desired. To file, go to *www.irs.gov* and search for Form 990-N ePostcard. Follow the links to the form. This return is very easy to complete and requires only a few pieces of information: legal name (and any other names used) and address of organization, employer ID number, tax year, name and address of a principal officer, website address if you have one, confirmation that income is less than $50,000, and notification in the case that an organization is going out of business.

This return does not require divulging the income of the organization, except that it is under $50,000. The e-postcard can be completed, and filing done in less than 10 minutes per year. With such a minimal effort required for small organizations to stay IRS-compliant, there are few good reasons to be revoked for not filing every year.

Form 990-PF
Return of Private Foundation or Section 4947(a) (1) Trust Treated as Private Foundation

Section 4947(a)(1) trusts are treated as private foundations. Form 990-PF is used to figure the tax based on investment income, and to report charitable distributions and activities.

HOW TO GET HELP

If you need help with filing, you can call IRS at 877-829-5500.

If you just want someone else to handle the filing for you, I highly recommend Darrell Hinch of *W. S. Hinch, Inc.*, a third-generation accountant who knows IRS nonprofit regulations inside and out, charges a fair price, and works quickly. How do I know? Of all the accountants in the United States, he is my accountant. Because he is dealing with IRS tax-exempt law, it is the same in every state, so it doesn't matter where you live. He can still help you with your IRS filings.

He can be reached at (636) 586-5258 or by email at *darrell@wshinch.com* or his website at *www.wshinch.com*

> **NOTE:** He has no idea I am recommending him, and I get no tangible gain of any kind from the referral. I would just like to make sure you get qualified service by a proven professional, so it is my pleasure to refer you to Darrell.

WHEN TO FILE

The filing deadline with IRS depends on the fiscal year of the organization. Filing due date is 4 ½ months after the fiscal year end. There is an extension possible for most forms, just like for individual income tax returns.

If an organization's fiscal year ends December 31, their Form 990, 990-EZ, 990-PF, or 990-N is due by May 15th of the following year. The extension for Form 990, 990-EZ, or 990-PF is until November 15th. No extensions are given for Form 990-N but you can still file it online for the remainder of the year and IRS doesn't normally say anything about it. To get an extension for 990, 990-EZ, or 990-PF, you must file IRS Form 8868, *Request for Extension of Time to File an Exempt Organization Return* to get a six-month extension. IRS will mail you a confirmation letter that your extension is approved, but it may take 6 – 8 weeks to arrive.

WISCONSIN

> **NOTE:** If you do not file and you do not request an extension, or you do not file by the end of the extension, IRS can send you a letter with a fine and $20 per day penalty. You can request they take away the fines and penalties by explaining your circumstances that caused you to file late, explaining that you are run by volunteers who are not savvy about tax filings, that you didn't know you had to file because your revenues were low or zero, and that you promise not to make the same mistake again now that you know you messed up. You are welcome.

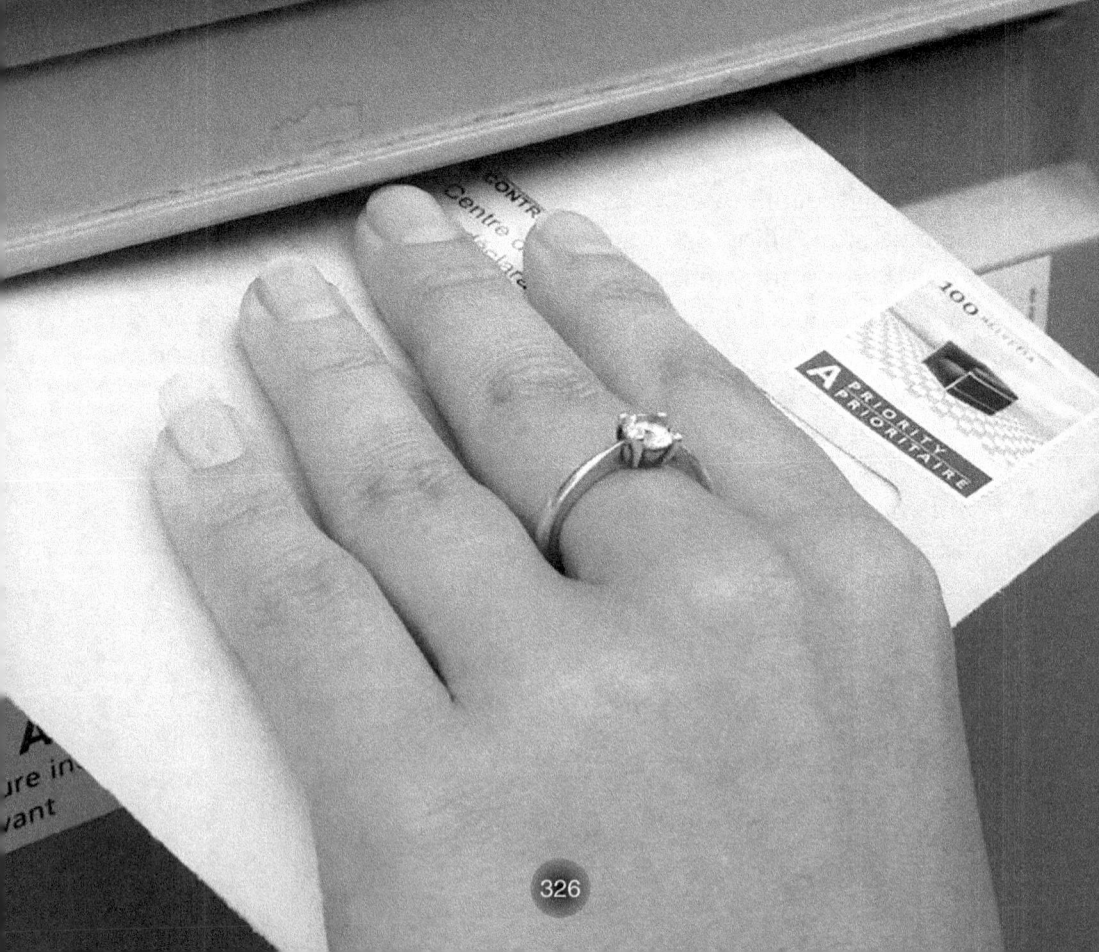

CHAPTER 36

APPLY FOR NONPROFIT STANDARD MAIL RATES

"To succeed you need to find something to hold on to, something to motivate you, something to inspire you."

—TONY DORSETT

Once you have nonprofit status with IRS, you may be able to get a nonprofit standard mail rate with the United States Postal Service. Eligible nonprofit organizations include religious, educational, scientific, philanthropic (charitable), agricultural, labor, veteran, and fraternal.

A responsible official from your organization must fill out United States Postal Service (USPS) PS Form 3624, *Application to Mail at Nonprofit Standard Mailing Rates*. You can get the form online, or you can get a copy of it at the post office. There will be some documents required to submit with the application. More information is contained in USPS Publication 417. You can view a copy online at *http://pe.usps.gov/text/pub417/welcome.htm*

Taking the time to get approved for nonprofit mailings can save a bunch on postage. The post office will weigh one item in your bundle of exact mailings and multiply by the number of items you are mailing. The rate is lower if you use a barcode on your mailing pieces and if they can be processed by machine instead of by hand. Talk with the post office about how to secure your newsletters or other mail pieces.

If you use staples to close a newsletter, your newsletters get torn in processing and can prohibit machining the mailing. Tape and postal seals work better and save on postage because they can be processed as machinable mail, saving significantly on every item.

It's best to talk with the postal workers who will actually process your nonprofit mailings before you send any out. They can give you all the discount information and all the requirements so you get your mailing ready correctly the first time, and they can show you examples of properly prepared bulk nonprofit mailings. Visit your local post office and ask to talk with someone who handles nonprofit bulk mailings.

SUMMARY

*"Never have a battle of wits with
an unarmed person."*

—Samuel Clemens (Mark Twain)

We hope this book has helped you navigate the often-tricky waters of government procedure and bureaucracy at state and federal levels. These rules and requirements exist to safeguard the public from fraud and scams, but for those of us who are hardworking, honest people, it may seem like overkill. Granted, applying for 501(c)(3) may not have been the easiest thing you ever did, but think about the result and the good you will do in the future because you completed the process now. We think you will agree it was worth the effort!

> **These rules and requirements exist to safeguard the public from fraud and scams**

We have tried to make the whole 501(c)(3) process simple from idea to reality by providing step-by-step guidance. We are also willing to answer specific questions for you as you go through the process. Please feel free to contact us at any time for additional help. You might also want to visit our websites at *www.taxexempt501c.com* or *www.doyourownnonprofit.com*

May God richly bless your efforts!

APPENDIX A

ACTUAL APPROVED NONPROFIT APPLICATIONS

DON'T REINVENT THE WHEEL!

One of the best parts of starting a nonprofit corporation is that you do not have to reinvent the wheel. If you know of a similar organization, you can request a copy of their Form 1023 with narrative. Wording on applications is not copyrighted, and if you see something you can use, tweak it to fit your organization instead of starting from scratch. Don't make it any harder than necessary.

We have included links to many approved nonprofit applications to help you get through the process. If you see one in this list that's similar to your organization, go to the website and review the application. All links worked at the time of publication.

All packages given are Forms 1023 prior to the 2020 revision of the form when IRS transitioned to online filings only, but the information is similar. Applications that contain the narratives are very helpful in understanding the kinds of information IRS wants to know to approve your application. We included a variety of nonprofits in the list to give you a wide assortment to choose from.

The budget information in the applications below ranges from $0 for brand new nonprofits just starting, up to budgets of hundreds of thousands of dollars or more. These are included to give you a broad range of examples. In addition, many also include their organizing documents and bylaws. Those organizational documents that contain the determination letter or other correspondence from IRS have been added after IRS completed their application. Your paperwork will not have those until IRS sends them after the fact.

West Hill Community Association
http://mywesthill.org/wp-content/uploads/2015/06/WHCA-501c3-Application.pdf

Chive Charities
https://chivecharities.org/uploads/pdfs/Form_1023.pdf

The Reno Initiative for Shelter and Equality
http://www.renoinitiative.org/wp-content/uploads/2014/03/FORM1023_3.1.13.pdf

Calapooia Food Alliance (Narrative only)
http://calapooiafoodalliance.org/papers/1023%20documents/Calapooia%20Food%20Alliance%201023%20attachment%205-01-09.pdf

Trek Continues, Inc.
http://www.duffylaw.org/tcaa.pdf

Friends of the Trumbull High School Choir, Inc.:
http://www.fothsci.org/uploads/5/2/4/9/5249683/fothsci_form_1023_application_for_recognition_of_exemption_-_501c3.pdf

The HAMS Harm Reduction Network, Incorporated:
http://hamsnetwork.org/corporate/f1023.pdf

Friends of Niger:
http://www.friendsofniger.org/pdf/FONTaxExemptApp.pdf

LegalCORPS:
http://legalcorps.org/wp-content/uploads/2012/01/1023-PubInspCopy.pdf

Minnesota Groundwater Association Foundation:
http://www.mgwa.org/foundation/documents/mgwaf-irs-1023.pdf

The Clear Fund:
http://www.givewell.org/files/ClearFund/Clear%20Fund%20Form%201023.pdf

Equipped to Survive Foundation, Inc.:
http://www.equipped.com/etsfi_form1023.pdf

The Light Millennium, Inc.:
http://www.lightmillennium.org/501_c_3/lmtv_form_1023.pdf

Software Freedom Conservancy, Inc.:
http://sfconservancy.org/docs/conservancy_Form-1023.pdf

A Grain of Hope Foundation, Inc.:
http://www.agrainofhope.org/form1023.shtml

Your Town Alabama, Inc.:
http://www.yourtownalabama.com/wp-content/uploads/2013/07/IRS-1023-Application-for-Recognition-of-Exemption.pdf

Playa del Fuego, Inc.:
http://playadelfuego.org/sites/default/files/boddocs/IRS-1023-complete.pdf

Other Applications that give a wider range of nonprofit examples:

The Creek Bed Foundation, a Charitable Trust:
http://thecreekbedfoundation.org/CreekBed1023.pdf

San Diego Speculative Fiction Society, Inc.:
http://www.sansfis.org/corporate_documents/IRS-1023/sansfis_irs1023.pdf

Husky Swimming Foundation (Also shows good wording to expedite application):
http://www.huskyswimmingfoundation.com/wp-content/HSF_Form1023.pdf

The Cordoba Initiative:
http://www.investigativeproject.org/documents/misc/435.pdf

Gaskov Clerge Foundation (GCF):
http://www.gaskov.org/Documents/Completed%20990%20Forms/GCF501C3%20%20%20501c3.pdf

Society of King Charles the Martyr, Inc.:
http://www.skcm-usa.org/Legal/SKCMForm1023asFiled.pdf

Grandfather Mountain Stewardship Foundation, Inc.:
http://www.grandfather.com/wp-content/uploads/2011/06/Application-for-Recognition-of-Exemption-Under-Section-501c3.pdf

Mozilla Foundation:
http://static.mozilla.com/foundation/documents/mf-irs-501c3-application-form-1023.pdf

Cadasil Together We Have Hope Nonprofit Organization:
http://cadasilfoundation.net/1023%20Original%20%20 Application%20for%20Website.pdf

Dianetics Foundation International:
http://www.xenu-directory.net/documents/corporate/irs/1993-1023-dfi.pdf

Wayland Public Schools Parent Teacher Organization, Inc.:
http://waylandpto.org/wp-content/uploads/2012/08/Form-1023.pdf

Multiple Sclerosis Foundation, Inc.:
http://990online.com/docs/5/592792934_87_1023.pdf

CAIRN Rescue USA:
http://www.cairnrescueusa.com/docs/CRUSA_1023.pdf

United States Australian Football League, Inc.: https://usafl.com/files/USAFL%20Form%201023%20Exemption%20Application.PDF

Trinity Mission Works, Inc.:
http://www.trinitymissionworks.org/Documents/IRS%20 1023%20ap.pdf

No Form 1023, but good Narrative section worthy of including:

San Francisco-Krakow Cities Association:
http://www.polishclubsf.org/Summary.pdf

APPENDIX B

STATES WITH STATUTORY PROVISIONS SATISFYING THE REQUIREMENTS OF INTERNAL REVENUE CODE SECTION 508(E).

The following states have adopted legislation satisfying the requirements of Section 508(e) relating to private foundation governing instruments. Information derived from Revenue Ruling 75-38, 1975-1 C.B. 161.

ALABAMA — except where otherwise provided by a decree of a court of competent jurisdiction or by a provision in the private foundation's governing instrument, which in either case has been entered or made after October 1, 1971, and expressly limits the applicability of state law.

ALASKA — except for such private foundations that expressly provide in their governing instruments that the applicable sections of Alaska law don't apply to them.

ARKANSAS — except for such private foundations which expressly provide in their governing instruments that the applicable sections of Arkansas law don't apply to them and except in the case of trusts where otherwise provided by decree of a court of competent jurisdiction.

CALIFORNIA — except where otherwise provided by a court of competent jurisdiction.

COLORADO — with respect to trusts that are private foundations except where otherwise provided by a court of competent jurisdiction.

CONNECTICUT — except where otherwise provided by a court of competent jurisdiction.

DELAWARE — except for such private foundations, which expressly provide in their governing instruments that the applicable sections of Delaware law don't apply to them.

DISTRICT OF COLUMBIA — except for such corporations, which expressly provide in their governing instruments that the applicable sections of District of Columbia law don't apply to them and except in the case of trusts where otherwise provided by a court of competent jurisdiction. (For purposes of this statute, corporations include corporations organized under any Act of Congress applicable to the District of Columbia as well as corporations organized under the laws of the District of Columbia.)

FLORIDA — except for such trusts that file a proper election not to be subject to the applicable provisions of Florida law and for such corporations as to which a court of competent jurisdiction has otherwise determined.

GEORGIA — except for such private foundations that file a proper election not to be subject to such law.

HAWAII — no exceptions.

IDAHO — except for such private foundations that expressly provide in their governing instruments that the applicable sections of Idaho law don't apply to them.

ILLINOIS — except for such corporations that have express provisions to the contrary in their articles of incorporation and except for trusts where it is otherwise provided by a court of competent jurisdiction.

INDIANA — except where otherwise determined by a court of competent jurisdiction with respect to private foundations organized before January 1, 1970.

IOWA — except for such private foundations which expressly provide in their governing instruments that the applicable sections of Iowa law don't apply to them.

KANSAS — except where otherwise provided by a court of competent jurisdiction.

KENTUCKY — except, with respect to corporations in existence on July 1, 1972, to the extent that such a corporation provides to the contrary by amendment to its articles of incorporation adopted after July 1, 1972, and, with respect to trusts in existence on July 1, 1972, where action is properly commenced on or before December 31, 1972, in a court of competent jurisdiction to excuse the trust from compliance with the requirements of section 508(e) of the Code.

LOUISIANA — except for such private foundations that expressly provide in their governing instruments that the applicable sections of Louisiana law don't apply to them.

MAINE — except where otherwise provided by a court of competent jurisdiction.

MARYLAND — except where otherwise provided by a court of competent jurisdiction.

MASSACHUSETTS — except where otherwise provided by a court of competent jurisdiction.

MICHIGAN — with respect to trusts that are private foundations except for such private foundations which file a notice of inconsistency under Michigan law.

MINNESOTA — except for private foundations that have been held by a court of competent jurisdiction not to be affected by such state statute.

MISSISSIPPI — except where otherwise provided by a court of competent jurisdiction.

MISSOURI — except for private foundations that have been held by a court of competent jurisdiction not to be affected by such state statute.

MONTANA — except in the case of trusts where otherwise provided by court decree entered after March 28, 1974, and except in the case of a corporation that has an express provision to the contrary in its articles of incorporation.

NEBRASKA — except for such trusts that effectively elect to be excluded from the applicable sections of Nebraska law, for such corporations which have governing instruments expressly providing to the contrary, and except as a court of competent jurisdiction has otherwise determined in any given case.

NEVADA — no exceptions.

NEW HAMPSHIRE — except where it is otherwise provided by a court of competent jurisdiction.

NEW JERSEY — except for such private foundations that expressly provide in their governing instruments that the applicable sections of New Jersey law don't apply to them.

NEW YORK — except where such law conflicts with any mandatory direction of an instrument by which assets were transferred prior to June 1, 1971, and such conflicting direction hasn't been removed legally.

NORTH CAROLINA — except for such private foundations which expressly provide in their governing instruments that the applicable sections of North Carolina law don't apply to them and except for trusts that have their governing instruments reformed by a decree of the Superior Court of North Carolina.

NORTH DAKOTA — with respect to trusts that are private foundations except where otherwise provided by a court of competent jurisdiction.

OHIO — except in the case of trusts where it is provided otherwise by a court of competent jurisdiction and except in the case of corporations in existence on September 17, 1971, which expressly adopt contrary provisions in their governing instruments after September 17, 1971.

OKLAHOMA — except for such private foundations that file a proper election not to be subject to such law.

OREGON — no exceptions.

PENNSYLVANIA — except where otherwise provided by a court of competent jurisdiction.

RHODE ISLAND — except where otherwise provided by a court of competent jurisdiction.

SOUTH CAROLINA — except for private foundations that expressly provide in their governing instruments that the applicable sections of South Carolina law don't apply to them.

SOUTH DAKOTA — except where otherwise provided by a court of competent jurisdiction.

TENNESSEE — except where otherwise provided by a court of competent jurisdiction.

TEXAS — except for such private foundations that a proper election not to be subject to such law.

UTAH — with respect to trusts that are private foundations except where otherwise provided by a court of competent jurisdiction.

VERMONT — except where otherwise provided by a court of competent jurisdiction.

VIRGINIA — except for private foundations whose governing instruments contain express provisions to the contrary or that have filed a proper election not to be subject to such law.

WASHINGTON — except for such private foundations that expressly provide in their governing instruments that the applicable sections of Washington law don't apply to them.

WEST VIRGINIA — with respect to trusts that are private foundations except for such trusts which provide in their governing instruments that the applicable sections of West Virginia law don't apply to them.

WISCONSIN — except as may otherwise be provided by decree of a court of competent jurisdiction.

WYOMING — except where otherwise provided by a court of competent jurisdiction.

Note from the Publisher

Are you a first time author?

Not sure how to proceed to get your book published?
Want to keep all your rights and all your royalties?
Want it to look as good as a Top 10 publisher?
Need help with editing, layout, cover design?
Want it out there selling in 90 days or less?

Visit our website for some exciting new options!

www.chalfant-eckert-publishing.com

www.ingramcontent.com/pod-product-compliance
Lightning Source LLC
Chambersburg PA
CBHW070046080526
44586CB00013B/929